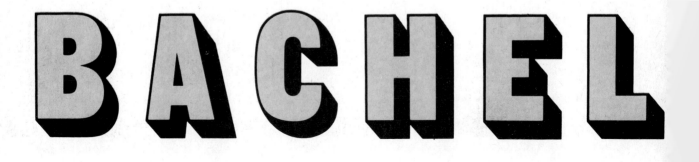

First published in Great Britain by **Sphere Books Ltd 1984**
30-32 Gray's Inn Road, London WC1X 8JL
Copyright © 1984 by Ben Elton, Rik Mayall and Lise Mayer

A Terence Blacker Book
Design by **Neville Brody**
Photographs by **Sheila Rock**

Second Impression

TRADE
MARK

Printed and bound in Finland *by WSOY*

ISBN 0 7221 5765 7

OR BOYS

THE YOUNG ONES BOOK

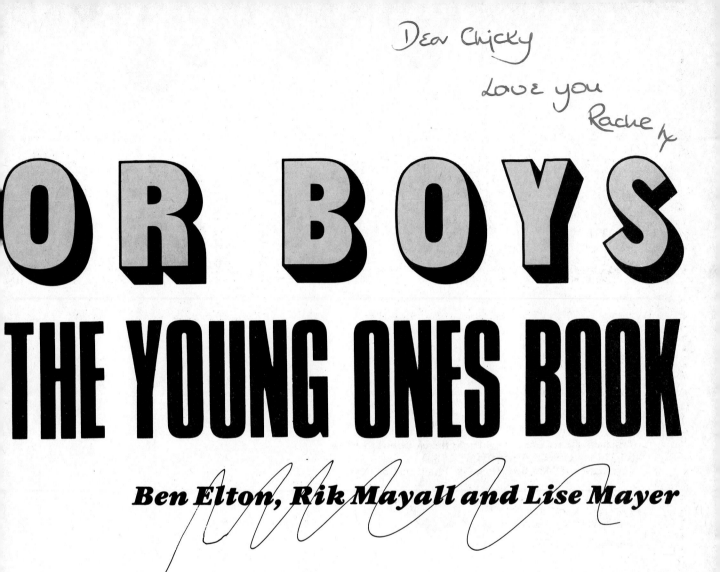

Ben Elton, Rik Mayall and Lise Mayer

Rik   Viv   Mike   Neil

SPHERE BOOKS LIMITED
London and Sydney

INTRODUCTION

by H.R.H. Charles, Prince of Wales

Hello. I'm the Prince of wales and anyone who says I'm not is a liar. And if you don't beleive me then you can bog off can't you because I've got a crown and everything to prove it and they fit I haven't just stolen them or anything like that ok? My mum is the Queen too so I wouldn't start acting ~~cleve~~ i clever if I was you not if you want to hang on to your goolies anyway. My grate friends the Young Ones especially Vyvyan who is a briliant bloke and who I'm going to knight as soon as I get the chance and I'm not lying have asked me to write an introduction to their completely brilliant book which ought to win all the book awards going particularly Vyv's bits which are absolutely f~~uckin~~ staggering in a literary sense.

You know, being the President of the World Wildlife FUnd or whatever I'm president of I often get asked the question, 'Princie? Did you see The Young ones on the telly last night?' and you know I always say, 'Yes I Did. Briliant wasn't it?' and that's true. And I also usually say Vyvyan was the best wasn't he? Because he is. All the others except Mike really are weedy nob ends and I'd run them down but I don't ~~xxxxx~~ want my Anglia getting dirty.

So there you have it. Read this book because I'm the prince of Wales and what I say goes, alright?

Love from,

H·R·H· PRINCE CHARLES.

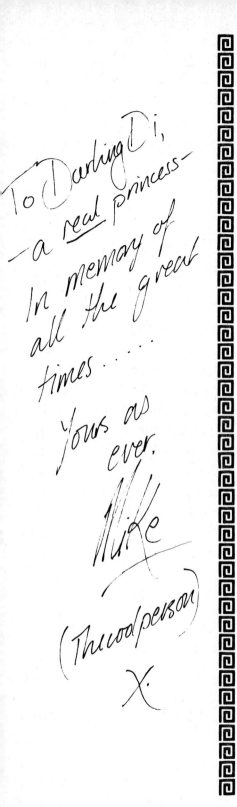

To Darling Di,
— a real princess —
In memory of
all the great
times . . . . .

Yours as
ever.

Mike
(Thewodperson)

X.

Foreword.
An apology

by Rick

Dear reader, any sexist, racist or politically unsound material in this book was written by Vyvyan, Mike and Neil. It has absolutely nothing whatever to do with me, although I did do most of the work – well I'm the most creative let's face it and I don't mean my nob. So all the really wacky, zany, crazy, anarchic, establishment-shattering, mind-numbing, bum-biting, bed-wettingly brilliant stuff in the book is by me. I'm certain the others would wish me to apologise on their behalf for everything else.

Four Words.
An apology

by Neil

I'm really really sorry.

Editor's glossary of terms

A note: Dear reader, as this 'book' is a young person's pop music pin-up sort of affair, those of you of a slightly more mature state of mind may find it all rather confusing. The following glossary is therefore designed to assist you on your ramblings through the strange twilight world of the young adult. I would also like to take this opportunity to thank my dear wife for her advice and suggestions as to the meaning of many of these words. Happy reading.

VIBES ● A musical instrument consisting of long tubular bells

GOOD VIBES ● A more expensive version of the same

HEAVY VIBES ● Again the same instrument, but an enormous model

TOTAL ● A type of petrol or oil

FREAK ● A deformed Victorian circus entertainer

TOTAL FREAKOUT ● A mass strike involving all the deformed Victorian circus entertainers over petrol prices

TOTAL MINDF✳✳K ● Someone has just inserted an oily penis into my ear

REALLY NEAT ● Good handwriting

GET IT ON ● For Heaven's sake hurry up and get dressed

AMAZING ● Pronounced amaaaaayyyzing, this seems to be a meaningless word employed to cover up a yawn during a conversation

TOTALLY AMAZING ● A difficult one, this. My wife suggests that it is a phrase used by a person who finds the subject of oil prices very dull. An Arab perhaps?

FAR OUT ● I am on a lilo and the current is rather strong (presumably)

LET'S SWEAR!

AN INTRODUCTION:

Swearing is really great as everyone who is cool knows. It makes you look really hard and grown-up. Yes, in this case it's actually **good** to look grown-up because it freaks out parents, pigs etc to see one of their number swearing when they all claim they don't and obviously do all the time because they're all liars and squares. Right, kids?

Swearing also impresses girls a lot because it makes you look as if you don't care whether you live or die and might very well smoke a whole packet of fags in one go and make yourself sick on purpose. It is also medically proven that swearing a lot makes your nob get bigger* which is very important.

I have therefore devised an easy to follow step-by-step guide to help even the biggest nerdy-nose (see how I slip them in?) look street and cool.

STAGE ONE

Before you can swear successfully you must know some rude words. It is very difficult to offend people with words like 'Hullo' or 'Do you take sugar?' Some words are ruder than others so how about it, kids? How about I just throw you in at the deep end with the real shockers?

Bum	**Nob**
Bits	**Wick**
Boob	**Cheeks**
Hole	**Pants**
Jobbie	**Thatcher**
Fart	

You can practice these words in the privacy of your own toilet (another potentially rude word). When you have been in the toilet by yourself for a while you may feel your confidence begin to swell. Nothing can stop you now. Try the words out on your Mum, teacher or any square handy. If you get caned or your mummy hits you on the bot with a slipper you're ready for **STAGE TWO.**

STAGE TWO

As you will have discovered by now, **They** don't like the kids to swear—yeah, mind control, 1984, all happening now. We are children of the recession—hard, street, uncontrollable with daggers in our eyes and up our bots. So let's face it, nerdies—yes that's right I JUST DON'T CARE—you may be feeling pretty chuffed with yourselves for calling teacher a square or dropping the odd fart into the conversation, but you're a zero swearily speaking until you can cope with 'THE DOUBLE'. TRY THESE FOR SIZE!!

And remember—all you need is a hyphen.

Poo-hole
Gas-leak pants
Toilet-trousers
Farty-breath
Nose-pick brain
Snot-face
Pizza-face
Ugly-face
Stupid-ugly-bastard-face fascist

*Prof J B Strangetrousers *Swearing a Lot Makes Your Nob Get Bigger* (Oxford University Press, 1933) £17.99

"Squares don't swear"—write it on your sociology file now!!!

Nob-face **

Jumbo-Jobbie (As in 'Oh Blimey, who's done a J-J on the sofa?' 'That's not a Jumbo-jobbie Rick, that's Neil watching the telly')

Bloody heck

Utter bastard (also complete, stupid-, great-brown-trousered)

Bum-wipe

hippy-pants

nob juice

Tebbit-breath

streaky-pants

That-cher

STAGE THREE

This is it—the Armageddon of Swearing. So fasten your seat-belts and write your will and don't bother to leave your old Bob Dylan records to me 'cos this cat's not into that reactionary nose-pick juice. No blummen way. I'm a passenger on the Rebel Express where the only place to put your pants is on your head.

FLUENT SWEARING BY A BILINGUAL HETERO TIGER:

Hey Twat-face nob off before I do a jobbie on your Heseltine!

Are you looking for a punch in the poo-hole Smeg-face?

Bloody heck you're a real stupid-ugly-bastard-face fascist aren't you?

I'll stick your pissy Goebbels up your junta in a minute, farty-breath!

Oi dribbly cheeks stop farting or I'll give you a bum-wipe to remember!

**Be careful – this could be construed as a compliment, unlike diarrhoea-face which could not.

farted?

Here's a puzzle for you, reader. Below is reproduced the sort of scene that is happening constantly round our place. Rick has detected a horrible farty smell and wants to know who farted but perhaps he is really trying to cover up the fact that it came from his bottom! Your job, reader, is to follow the scene and try and work out 'WHO FARTED'.

THE JOY OF SHOPING

Power. Shoping is like a really important thing that HAS TO BE DONE like almost every month. It's so important that you have to organise a ROTA to make sure the whole scene actually happens. Here's an example of our shoping rota:

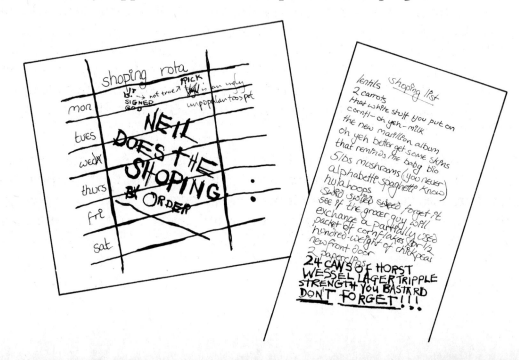

As you can see, in our house I have to take it in turns with myself to do the shoping. This is because:

a Rick objects to all financial transactions on moral grounds.

b If you so much as mention shops to Vyvyan, he forces you to eat furniture.

c Mike 'never does the shoping you know that, Neil'.

Nevertheless, it's a ruthlessly efficient system and one thing it has got going for it is that you never have to get into boring arguments about whose turn it is to go shoping. This gives you more time to have boring arguments about the much more important subject of WHO'S GOING TO PAY.

It's best to get into this argument about three to four hours before you like actually want to leave for the shops because the average shoping bill being about fifteen billion pounds and ninety-nine new pee, most breadheads would rather kill than cough up the cash.

There are several ways of deciding whose turn it is to pay for the shoping:

1 **FIGHTING** All the members of the house hit each other with their fists, crockery and other members of the house until all but one are lying on the floor going, 'Oh God . . .', 'Oh wow Vyvyan you've broken my arm . . .', 'Help me, I can't see properly', 'Where are my teeth' etc, etc.
Result: I pay for all the gear.

2 **DEMOCRACY** Each member of the house stands up simultaneously and shouts, 'It's Neil's turn to pay the bill because he's such a lazy tightfisted health-risk and anyway Neil there's three of us and we've voted already that it's your turn, Neil or don't you believe in democracy Neil? I suppose you'd rather be living in Nazi Germany and forcing the working class to go to the shops for you, wouldn't you? Well I've got news for you Herr Neil Goeballs – we won the war forty years ago so shut-up, dust off your purse and get down to Sainsbury's. God he makes me baity.'
Result: I pay for all the gear.

3 **BALLOT** There are like three kinds of ballot. The postal ballot, where everyone writes the word 'Neil' on a piece of paper and sticks it through the letterbox; the secret ballot, where everyone goes to their bedrooms and writes 'Neil' on a piece of paper and then comes back to the living room and reads it out; and the mass meeting, where everyone stands up, sticks their right hand in the air and shouts 'Neil'.
Result: I pay for all the gear. Again.

The only slightly heavy thing about this is like when you haven't got any bread. It's more than slightly heavy really, I mean it's like a mega-hassle because if you tell your flatmates you've got no cash they just don't believe you and like real physical bad news occurs with fists and bottles etc. But if you truck out to the shop and truck back with like zero groceries because you're so breadless, your flatmates' reaction could quite easily see you into hospital. So it's like a real cleft stick (which can be really useful for finding water at festivals) and the only way out is even more dangerous – you've got to STEAL.

Like, the choice is simple. You either steal the gear from the shop, or steal the bread to buy the gear. THERE IS NO OTHER WAY. So which to choose?

STEALING? RIGHT ON!

'Why do I steal? I steal to eat. Why do I eat? I eat to live. Why do I live? I live to die. Why do I die? Because I feel like it that's why – So don't fence me in Daddio, ask me when I'm gone.'

These were the words of my famous ancestor, the legendary shoplifter, poet and revolutionary Rick Turpin, speaking at his trial at Newgate, shortly before he was sentenced to be hung by the neck until dead.

'Oh please Your Majestic Honour, it wasn't me, it was the others, I didn't do it, they made me, honestly, it wasn't me, hang them.'

These were the words of Rick's famous ancestor, the legendary shoplifter, poet and revolutionary at his trial at Newgate, shortly after he was sentenced to be hung by the neck until dead.

STEALING FROM THE GUYS – THE PROS AND CONS

The pros
1 I know where they live.

The cons
1 The guys never have any money.
2 You get caught.
3 You have to go to hospital.
4 You still have to do the shoping.

Vyvyan **Reagan**

SHOPLIFTING COMPETITION

Take two incidents:

a President Reagan floating mines into a peaceful Nicaraguan port.
b Vyvyan nicking a packet of Toffo's from Mr McNobby's girly mag shop.
One of these incidents resulted in a five pound fine, and ten bangs on the bot with the slipper. The other provoked mild rebuke.
Can you tell which got which?

THE JOY OF SHOPLIFTING

The supermarket

A supermarket is bad vibesville deluxe for freaks. There is nothing super about it, and come to think of it nothing much market about it either. I mean if you and your old lady were to go down there to score some afghani carpet coats or even some crushed velvet loons you'd be there all night except that like they're closed at night and anyway you'd probably split after like about four seconds because the vibes are so uncool. Even the sounds there are totally straight-orientated.

Shoplifting-wise they're a total bummer 'cos the head breadhead's troops all hang out in white coats and hit you with heavy rap numbers like can I help you sir you seem to be looking for something just when you're about to slip some muesli into your sock. But the worst thing about supermarkets is the lack of privacy. You may not know this, but when you go into a supermarket you are on TV – yeah I know that's a pretty mind-numbing concept, 1984, thought police an' all that but it's for real. Glance at the ceiling next time you're there if you don't believe me. So like not only are there scores of pigs and secret pigs watching your every move, but millions of viewers and maybe even your mum. So like besides all the bread hassles you've been having anyway just to score some shoping you have to get even more bread together to get some decent rags together in case some mega-talent scout is watching. My advice is make like a drum – beat it.

THE JOY OF SHOPING ★

The cornershop

When you first try shoplifting in a corner shop you think hey wow this is more like it. Usually only one grocer man or lady and they're usually pretty untogether muscle-wise, but there are two main disadvantages: 1) the only gear you can reach easily is stuff like gobstoppers and penny assortments and the guys get pretty uncool when they get wine gum cassoulet for tea more than three times a week, 2) watch out for loaded double barrel shotguns behind counter – this is really uncool and should you find yourself looking down the barrel – make like a banana – split.

Machines

Shoplifting from machines is the pits – you have to put some bread in the slot before you can steal any gear. Don't make like an elephant – forget it.

Headshops

It may be hard for a hipster to swallow – oh very funny Rick like thanks for telling me that joke about things being hard to swallow again – but shoplifting-wise a headshop is manna from Nirvanah. As well as being full of really grate gear like lentils, chick peas, aduki beans, more lentils, tahini, dried black eyed peas, soya beans, lentils and useful household tools like – look shut up Rick all right – bongs, giant skins, joss-sticks and nepalese rice paintings – THEY ARE RUN BY FREAKS. If a freak catches you with a granola munchy bar down your jeans you just say hey man don't hassle me – are you like into material possessions and being a straight breadhead or what? If he responds by arresting you you can always threaten to tell the pigs about his mega red leb operation round the back, it never fails. So make like a rooster – suck seed.

there's nothing in the kitty.

I AM FAT, AND I LIKE IT
--→ VYVYAN SPEAKS OUT

Here is a picture of my tum, set against a picture of a hot air balloon

Can you spot the difference?
It isn't easy, is it? And why? Because I'm FAT! And it's grate!

- THINGS YOU CAN DO WITH A FAT TUM
  1 **Pretend to be BIG DADDY so that policemen will think twice before kicking you in the stomach.**
  2 **Fit more lager and curry in it.**
  3 **Roll up your shirt, flop it on the table and say 'what about that for a whopper mum?'**
  4 **Draw a line down the middle and pretend it's your bottom.**

- THINGS YOU CAN'T DO WITH A THIN TUM
  Any of the above

Thinny said to Fatty, 'Ooh, aren't you a slob?
Your tum is such a floppy one, it must obscure your knob.
Isn't that a problem, when you're on the job?'
Said Fatty, 'I'm a girly' and smashed him in the gob.

CRAFT ✄ CORNER

Mike stains a duvet

Has your mum bought you your first duvet? Looks pretty clean doesn't it? No way is that a sexy sack. Boys or girls, a spotless duvet means virgin city, which is a very unfashionable place to live. On the other hand collecting the genuine stains is not always to be recommended, there is now a real body of scientific evidence to suggest that there *is* a connection between banging away like an armed policeman, and PREGNANCY. So this is how you can look good, and feel sexy, without even knowing a member of the opposite sex. Ask your mum for some flour and a mixing bowl. Get some water, and mix it all up like glue. Then get your ruler out of your geom set, and flick lumps of the stuff at your duvet. The results will bring gasps of envious wonder from your friends.

Vyvyan mends the telly

Go up to telly and shout 'work you bastard'. If this doesn't work, throw set out of window. If it still won't cooperate start sawing its legs off one by one till it gives in. If this makes telly unstable prop it up with unsold copies of Neil's Book of the Dead.

Mike explains how to be a supergrass

Honour among thieves is all well and groovy, but it don't go for nothing when you're doing two hours detention. Let me put it this way, you're on the carpet, and your grant's on the line. The man has the evidence, piled on his desk are fifteen pieces of blank A4 where there should have been essays. This time, no parole, no '50 lines and don't do it again'. It's all the way to the dole queue for Mike the Cool Person. So what do you do? Simple, you do a deal, I'm standing there thinking, what do I have to sell? Well, Neil's soggy flannel with the dope seeds going mouldy should be worth something, and Vyvyan's stolen skeleton from the lab and Rick's nudey picture in his rough book. You want to get out of trouble, simple – squeal on your mates.

Neil explains how to smoke super grass

Well it's a bit difficult to explain really, you know, without showing you, so, well basically, if anyone's got any really super grass (or any grass at all for that matter) if they give me a call, I'd be happy to show them how to smoke it.

How to make your own pot

Pottery can only be done when all the other members of your commune are out or away for the weekend because like there's no way you want to get your own record player all manky. So sometimes, when a sudden urge to do a pot comes on, you have to get the guys out of the house yourself by casually dropping hints like, oh wow, get the fuck out of here everyone the house is on fire, or, oh no, I shouldn't have had that last lentil I think I can feel a cataclysmic biggie coming on. This will give you a couple of hours for what we potters call 'throwing' the pot (not to be confused with the traditional Glastonbury sport).

Here's how:

fig 1. **Get the record player together.**   *fig 2.* **Get the clay together.**   *fig 3.* **Get the pot together.**

See? Simple isn't it? The only hassle is if the guys believe your story about the fire and like call the pigs and when they rush in to look for the fire all they can find is you trying to close the lid of the record player and stuff it up your jumper and the head pig screams, 'What's in that stereo, Greenham-freak?' and you say only my pot and they smash it to pieces, examine it carefully and smash your face in for 'lying'. Then they smash the guys faces in for wasting police time, and the guys smash your face in for getting them beaten up. Then they smash your face in again for wrecking their record player, and getting clay all over the walls. So the safest way to make pots is to buy them from Sainsbury's.

(N.B. Never 'throw' your pot at 78 rpm.)

How to make your own bed

You will need:
1 A bed.
2 A bedroom.
3 Neil.

Making a bed is very simple. Here's how:

1 Stand at foot of bedstead.
2 Shout 'Come here at once Neil you disgusting hippy'.
3 Shout 'Neil, I've told you once already, if you're not here in three seconds I'll tell Vyvyan that it was you who messed up his bogey collection'.
4 Shout 'One . . . Two . . . Thr-'.
5 Whisper 'Neil, you little bastard you wouldn't dare tell Mike and Vyvyan about that – God, you spiteful little bastard!'
6 Make the bed.

ACCEPTABLE DESIGNS FOR YOUR COVERLET

UNACCEPTABLE DESIGNS FOR YOUR COVERLET

Neil's Underpant Garden

Power. A lot of groovers would love to be at one with the trees and the earth and the sky.

And it's no use Vyvyan shouting, 'No, they bloody wouldn't,' across the room at me, because this is my bit of the book and I'm doing it, so bad vibe on your loons, Vyvyan.

Anyway, as I was saying, many people would like to be at one with nature, but find it difficult because they live in SHITTY URBAN DECAY MAN. It's tough to be a total groover when the lift's broken and there's sick all over the stairs.

Inside each hooligan is a total groover. Outside each hooligan is eight trillion square miles of SHITTY URBAN DECAY MAN, the territory of **Lord Bad Vibe.**

Lord Bad Vibe says he doesn't dig hooligans right? but in fact man – HE DOES!!! Yeah, he does, and the reason is, that hooligans give him an excuse for . . . **MORE PIGS.**

Have you ever wondered why SHITTY URBAN DECAY MAN is so shitty? Surely it wasn't necessary to make inner city housing *that* bum? NO IT WASN'T. When Lord Bad Vibe first had the idea of building SHITTY URBAN DECAY MAN, he decided to make *it as bumly as possible.* For two reasons:
1. It would cost less, and
2. It would mean everyone would be really uptight, and aggressive, so he could win elections shouting 'Law and Order' and 'BUY MORE *PIGS!!!*'
Lord Bad Vibe loves pigs.

So what do you do?
Well, Vyvyan says smash Mrs Thatcher over the head with a brick, and Mike says become a criminal, and Rick says, 'Ooh er, well I'm sure Mr Kinnock's a very nice man', but I say, Lord Bad Vibe deliberately left out gardens when he built SHITTY URBAN DECAY MAN. Cool him out . . .

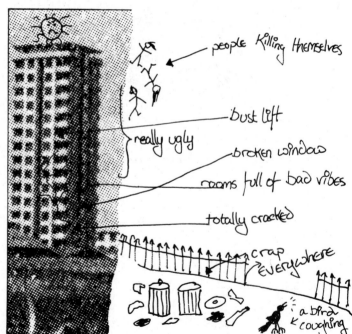

people killing themselves

really ugly

bust lift

broken windows

rooms full of bad vibes

totally cracked

crap everywhere

a bird coughing

Become a Gardener

You don't need a real garden man! You can make your own and here's how, with **NEIL'S UNDERPANT GARDEN.**

Become a grower. Become a groover. Become a gardener. You know how you tend to wear a pair of underpants for about a year then sling them out? Well, DON'T, because I have discovered that in this state, they make PERFECT GARDENS MAN!!! Just dampen them (if they're not damp already) and lay them out on the table in your bedroom man, and sow the seeds, it is TOTALLY AMAZING.

BY THE END OF ALL THIS, YOUR KARMA SHOULD BE COMPLETELY GROOVY, YOU OWN A GARDEN AND ANYTHING THAT YOU SHOULD DO IN THE GARDEN, YOU CAN NOW DO IN YOUR PANTS.

People, why can't we all like just be really you know like nice
because y'know, I mean the thing is right,   (sory that was a mistake)

wow this typewriter is kind of difficult to 18 get your head round
? riGht. People, why don't we I mean who can't we just get it together a
sorry.Hang on.
Look right, what I'm trying to say withot much help from this typeright
ok is that if the whole ~~hol~~ world would just ~~aaaaa shiit~~ mellow
out a bit we could ~~al~~be peaceful and beutiful children WHy won't the f
N work oN this thiNgoh it has typical even the typerighters got it in fo
if there were no automation and we oh wow i mean ~~wasa~~ no automation
and We were all freeto go as w7½ as we please~~aa shit~~
liStenYOU WoNT geT me misertyperighter hare Kri?hna hare rAma kri?hna kRi
i?na ~~aaaaa~~ kri? ? ?????? OHWOW WHOS?IS THIS THING EVERy time i pre??
~~aaaaa~~ the ? i get a ?   ?hit.

P
E
A
C
E

luv

magic

even the snail
leaks a stardust trail

i8ky me??

RIZLA

LEGALISE IT

'Hullo, mateys,' says Rick *(of TV's famous 'Whoops, my bottom's farted!'),* **'Aren't baths boring? But not anymore, with new 'MATEY' foam bath!'**

Remember that horrid moment when you've just started to 'wash' your private bits, and Mum comes in to discuss your homework? Well, with a 'MATEY' foam bath you can wash your willy as fast as you like, and mum need never know!

Matey helps you 'work up a lather' in more ways than one. Perhaps they should change its name from 'MATEY' to 'WANKY'. Right, kids?

Spot the difference

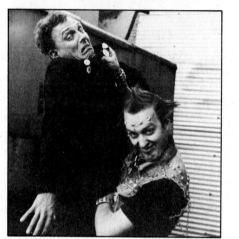

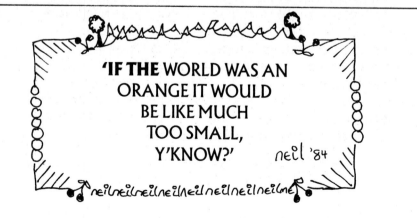

'IF THE WORLD WAS AN ORANGE IT WOULD BE LIKE MUCH TOO SMALL, Y'KNOW?'

neil '84

neilneilneilneilneilneilneilneilne

The history of POP

PART ONE

ROOTS

The story of pop music is basically the story of Cliff Richard, and vice versa. The two are identical, except, of course, pop music doesn't go out with Sue Barker.

From the beginning, Cliff had many imitators, perhaps the best known being the American cabaret artiste Elvis Presley. Elvis modelled his career on Cliff except of course, he didn't go out with Sue Barker. Elvis died in 1977, just one year after Cliff had invented punk rock. His last words were, 'Does anyone have any more hamburgers and drugs?'

But that's jumping ahead a little. Let's go back to the brief period of Cliff's life when he and Tommy Steele were negro slaves on an Alabama chain gang. It was the chance overhearing of all the other slaves singing lots of songs that they'd made up, that led Cliff to invent 'the blues'. Cliff waited until the evil slave overseer wasn't looking and then whispered to Tommy, 'Pssst! hey, why don't we combine "the blues" with elements of white country music, and call it "rock and roll".' There was an immediate glint in Tommy's eye as he turned and said, 'Sod off, I'm trying to write *Half a Sixpence.*'

And that's how it all started.

PARTY

MIKE SPEAKS OUT. Everybody has had one good party. You remember the one, when you *didn't* throw up red wine all over your new Santana album, or you *didn't* spend the whole evening trying to get off with someone who is actually physically allergic to you. And you *didn't* try to ignite one of your farts and end up setting fire to your trousers. And you *didn't* suddenly decide that the whole world was hollow and empty, like your life, and spend the whole evening sitting on the stairs getting out of people's way while they queue for the loo and hoping someone will come and say 'Hey what's wrong? have a bang on this number man'.

BASICALLY, the only good party is the one someone else holds that you don't go to. But if you do, here are some essential rules.

1 *Do not allow your room to be used as the 'Coats room'.* Coat room in party talk translates to 'snog room'. After all, where else do people get the chance to bonk on top of fifty-six bomber jackets and a snoopy bag? For months after the party you will be finding snogging couples hidden in the folds of your duvet. Two years later when you finally start to tidy up because you're moving out, you will unearth a couple of cobwebbed, emaciated figures, locked forever in an eternal circular dialogue:

HE: Look, please come back with me, just for coffee, I mean, really, I'm not, you know, trying anything on, it's just I *really* like you,

H I N T S

I think you're incredibly *interesting* to *talk* to, please, just for coffee.

SHE: Oh I don't know, I've got a nine-thirty lecture . . . . (The haunted houses of the next century will not be peopled by romantic cavaliers starved to death hiding from Roundheads, but by horrid, thin, third year maths students, endlessly trying to persuade plump first year Eng Lit girls to come home and fuck them).

2 If you're *going* to a party, never leave your coat in the coat room unless you want to arrive home with a pocket full of rubber johnnies.

3 *Do not carpet the toilet on the day before the party.* It is an interesting fact that all boys when getting ready to go to a party, along with the best shirt and the Eau Savage, seem to feel it necessary to attach a garden sprinkler to the end of their nobs. Nothing else can explain the lakes of piss which are the trademark of the party toilet.

4 *Never hold the wrong type of party.*

RIGHT TYPE OF PARTY
The one you cancel.

The one your fifteen-year-old sister holds, where you can be impressive, and try to get off with her mates.

WRONG TYPE OF PARTY
The Conservative party.

GLOSSARY OF TERMS USED TO DESCRIBE PARTIES

'Hi. Come in!': Who are you?

Booze is in the kitchen: There is a table of full empty bottles in the kitchen.

Punch: A large bowl of flat lemonade.

Sounds: A microscopic cassette tape recorder that doesn't work.

'Anyone fancy dancing?': 'For Christ's sake, stop fighting everybody, the police are on their way.'

'Whoops-a-daisy!': 'All right. Who threw the record player through the window?'

'It's going great, isn't it?': 'Do you need an ambulance?'

'I've cleaned it up and I think it's OK': There is a huge puddle of red wine sick on your stereo/duvet/dog.

'Coffee anyone?': 'I want you all to leave this very instant. It's been the worst party of my life and I'm on the brink of actually killing someone.'

DR MIKE 'THE COOL PERSON'

Dear Guys

VYVYAN BASTERD M.D.

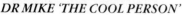

RICK — Even if they gave me an OBE I'd send it back (initials are for pigs and squares)

TOSSER →

NEIL PYE F.R.E.A.K.

LET THE EXPERTS HELP, ADVISE AND COMFORT YOU IN YOUR HOUR OF NEED

■ Dear Neil,
What can I do? My girlfriend has just left me a week before our wedding, saying that I'm dull, ugly and a total no-hoper. Before leaving she stole all my money and burnt my house down. Now the doctor tells me I have contracted a terminal disease. Help.
(GS, Lancs.)
**Dear Mr Lancs,
You think you've got problems. What about me? I wish *I* had a fatal disease, actually I probably do, not that anyone would care.**

■ Dear Rick,
This may sound silly but I really think I am going mad. I am desperately unhappy. I work by night as a security guard. I never see anyone. None of my friends like me any more. I cry all the time. What can I do???
Lonely (Herts)
**Dear Lonely,
You're right, your letter does sound bloody silly: didn't they teach you to punctuate properly at school or perhaps you were just too dim to learn. You deserve everything you get, fascist. If you want to wear a uniform so badly why don't**

you just go out and join the Nazi party? I'm not surprised none of your friends want anything to do with you – you sound like a horrid, nerdy-brained, pervy little Hitler and I've got a good mind to use your letter as lavvy paper except that I'd probably just catch some ghastly homosexual disease.

Dear Vyv,
This may sound silly but I really think I am going mad my courtiers won't obey me any more banana banana even my tailor has started making me stupid white canvas jackets logenberry that you have to wear back to front grateful for any advice.
Yours Emperor Napoleon Bonaparte I. (Broadmoor)
Dear Bonie Your Highness,
You are not mad. I suggest you invade Russia this winter.

MIKE'S QUICK ANSWER
Q: *My girlfriend complains that in six years she has never had an orgasm.*
What can I do?
A: **Sleep with her.**

Ref 453/2BN   L.E.B.
Customer accounts

F I N A L   D E M A N D
Our files show the remittance for the last quarter ending 6/8/84 is now 5 weeks overdue. If the balance is not settled by 20/11/84 we shall be forced to terminate your supply and start legal proceedings. Thank you for your attention.

Dear Electricity Board,
If you do not stop hassling us soon, we shall be forced to cut off your bollocks.
Yours sincerely,
'Auntie' Mike, the Cool Person.

P.S. I should like to apologise for the presumption that The Electricity Board is a man. This is a non sexist household and we will quite happily cut off your tits.
Yours sincerely, Leon Trotsky.

■ Dear Messrs Person and Trotsky,
The Electricity Board is not a man or a woman, it is a nationalised industry and hence has neither 'Bollocks' or 'Tits'. It does however, have about six trillion volts, which you will find up your bottom if you don't pay us sharpish.
Yours sincerely, *The Electricity Board.*

brilliant! when? love darth vader

■ Dear Messrs Person, Trotsky and Vader,
Just bloody pay the bill will you.

20.11.84

Dear 'leccy groovers,
Power. Look, I'm sorry but bread is very tight just now, how about if we tried this, I've got 8 new p in the dope emergency fund, and I can let you have say, 4p, then if I
like lay a really heavy scrounging and responsibility trip on the other guys, I might raise . . . O$_h$ ^{n}o, the ^l_ights have g$_o$$_n$$_e$$_o$$_u$ . . .

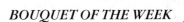

BOUQUET OF THE WEEK

Flowers are on their way to Mr P Thomas of Ipswich, Suff. His wife writes, *'Dear Guys, my husband was a complete bastard so last Wednesday I killed him. I don't want to waste a load of good cash buying flowers for the funeral, but the police might get suspicious if I don't send a wreath.'*

Enjoy your flowers, Mr Thomas.

LAV GA

*t*oilets are great. Toilets are a guy's best friend–who else can you turn to when you've just had a Special Fried Rice and ten pints of lager? Not your dog, that's for sure–think of the cleaning bill. And you know, when you're alone, sitting on the old lavvy with your trousers round your ankles (and your pants of course, don't forget) there's nothing I like better than a good hard lavvy game. And there's loads to choose from.

One of my big faves is 'Change the words of the pop-song'. What you do is pick a song and change the words. (NB: Not all of them, it's too easy then–you get things like 'I'm the leader of the gang I am' changing to 'Poo bum wobble-botty nob nob sex'. See? Too easy.) The game is also supposed to be on the raunchy side a bit, so let's open with an easy example that always goes down well with rude joke fans: changing the word 'love' to 'lav' (CHORTLE). Have a go yourself, but in the meantime here's a few I've thought up: 'Baby, baby, where did our lav go?' (Supremes there, of course), ' ... and the moment that I feel that you

feel that way too (sounds dirty already, eh readers?) is when I fall in (the) lav with you,' (Natty King Cole) and lots more ('Stoned in lav with you'–one for Neil there–'Baby Lav', 'I Want Your Lav' etc etc).

A great laugh of course, but this is only the BEGINNING. Much more adventurous is the Mark II version of the game, where you insert a dirty word of your choice ANYWHERE YOU LIKE in a song. It's utterly brilliant fun honestly. Look, I'll show you. Let's take the word FART (I should have chosen the word nob shouldn't I readers? then I could have written a bit of a song and then put 'Insert your nob here!!! I could have done that, couldn't I? and it would have been brilliant and great, but I think that's a wee bit anarchic even for me! Blimey, you must all think I'm absolutely potty and wild some of the things I say, mustn't you? Well, I suppose I am really, sometimes I'll just do anything to make people laugh. Anything at all, I just don't care!!!! The other day, right, don't ask me why, we were all in the sitting room and all of a sudden I leapt up and shouted, 'Look

MES

out, I'm a Duran Duran record,' and I sat on the record player and started singing 'Reflex' in a really stupid voice! It was so funny! Everybody thought so. Well, some of the guys didn't quite get it, but Neil was watching. It was pretty tricky keeping a straight face too I can tell you, especially as the prong in the middle of the turntable was sticking right up my bot and made my eyes water quite a bit and left a nasty bruise. But the guys didn't know what to say. I finished the song and went up to my bedroom to COMPLETE SILENCE. BRILLIANT!)

Anyway, back to Mark II of the game, here are some examples of randomly inserted farts, and they really are a scream:

'The fart cats' *(The Cure)*
'Born to be farty' *(Steppenwolf)*
'Dance away the fart-ache' *(Roxy Music)*
'Pretty farty' *(Sex Pistols)*
'London's farting' *(Clash)*
'My name is Michael Fart . . .' *(Madness)*
'Bad Fart Rising' *(Creedence Clearwater Revival)*
'When a man loves a Fart' *(Percy Sledge)*
'Let's Fart' *(David Bowie)*
'Saturday Night's alright for Farting' *(Elton John)*
'F.A.R.T.I.N.G.' *(Tammy Wynette)*
'Farter' *(Michael Jackson)*
'It's my party and I'll fart if I want to . . . ' *(Brian Ferry etc)*
'Street-farting Man' *(Stones)*
'The fart is mine' *(Michael Jackson/Paul McCartney)*
'I feel like a fart-machine' *(James Brown)*

'**Farty woman**' *(Roy Orbison)*
'**Your fart's too big**' *(Fats Waller)*
'**They call me farty-pants**' *(The Chiffons)*
'**Come on baby light my fart**' *(The Doors)*
'**Last train to Fartsville**' *(Monkees)*
'**Hey, big farter**' *(Shirley Bassey) (Plus* '**Fartfinger**' *and* '**Farts are forever**')
'**House of the rising fart**' *(Animals)*
'**Do ya think I'm farty?**' *(Rod Stewart)*
'**Farty Christmas**' *(Slade)*
'**Nobody told me there'd be farts like these, strange farts indeed** *(John Lennon)*
'**. . . when you think I've farted all I can, I'm gonna fart just a little bit more**'
(Dr Hook)
'**Fart!**' *(Lulu)*
'**Farty talk**' *(Captain Sensible)*
'**Whole lotta farting going on**' *(Jerry Lee Lewis)*
'**Bad farts**' *(Wham)*
'**Stray Cat Fart**' *(The Stray Cats)*
'**Twist and fart**' *(The Beatles)*
'**Don't fart so close to me**' *(Police)*
'**Fart away the heartache**' *(Roxy Music)*
'**My fart**' *(Frank Sinatra)*
'**Robert DeNiro's farting**' *(Bananarama)*

Well, I bet you've all pissed yourselves playing that game and the great thing is IT DOESN'T MATTER—'cos you're SITTING ON THE LAV!!!!!!! Brilliant—you can say to your friends, 'Hey I played a game last night that was so funny I actually pissed myself', and when they say, 'Blimey, that was a bit anarchic—but what about your trousers?' you can say—'Oh, I wasn't wearing any!' Amazing.

There's practically no limit to what you can do in the lav—depending on how big your lav is of course! Hey, here's a good joke: 'Why did the company director stick his head down the lavvy?'. 'He wanted to keep an eye on his business'—I just made that up—honestly! 'Why was Paul McCartney depressed when he looked in the toilet?'. 'Because he'd gone from number one to number two!!!!!!!' 'Why are toilets good for the unemployed?' ''Cos there are always lots of jobbies there!' I JUST DON'T CARE! A word of warning however—Achtung! Oh no, there I go *again*—no, seriously kids, there are some games I would not recommend in the lav—tennis, hopscotch, double-dutch, hide and seek and monopoly—for the obvious reason—ie it would be too easy to cheat. Hey Ho—well I could go on all night – and sometimes do when I've had a curry! There's really no end to things to do on the lav – flick the bogie, sweepstake derby on how many flops you're going to do (a bit unwise after a heavy curry), sink-the-fag-end and, of course, seek the lavatory paper, to name but a few. The other great thing to do in the lav if you are of artistic bent (yes ha bloody ha) is GRAFFITI. Writing on walls is hard and cool and has lots of street credibility (unless you are Neil, Mike or Vyvyan). It might not bring down the government, but if you press hard enough it might bring down the wall (and if you live next door to Thatcher and she suddenly saw you sitting on the lavvy with your pants round your ankles and your spray gun in your hand she might have a heart attack and die). So remember the motto, 'It is better to Write on the Wall than Shit in your Pants'.

NEIL'S TEN COMMANDMENTS

1 Thou shalt not get really uncool and violent with me just because I couldn't get the supper together on time because I'm going through a bit of a depression at the moment.

2 Thou shalt not criticise flares and call people who wear them an unfashionable spazmo all the time.

3 Thou shalt not slam my head in the fridge door.

4 Thou shalt not scratch all my Grateful Dead records and set fire to my record player 'for a joke'.

5 Thou shalt do the washing up just once, just for a change to see what a really disgusting thing it is and how nobody ever does it but me ever.

6 Thou shalt not sneak into my room and biro 'Meat eater' on my forehead, the night before my animal rights meeting.

7 Or 'I dig Thatcher, smash my face in'.

8 Nor shalt thou tie me down and superglue cornflakes round my mouth before my new girlfriend, the only one I've ever had, comes round and then when she does shout 'Look out, the hippy's got herpes!'.

9 Never eat your ~~...~~

10 ~~...~~

USEFUL HOUSEHOLD HINTS

How to deal with . . .

Fish in the television set: Tie a bent pin to the end of a bit of string and put a maggot on the pin. Dangle down the back of television set. When you feel a 'tug' on the string, withdraw it from television and remove fish from pin. Repeat process until all fish have been caught.

Bird droppings under the carpet: Untack carpet and fold back to reveal stain. Ensure that stain is completely dry, and brush with stiff brush, mark should disappear completely. Replace, and tack down carpet.

A hot water pipe that goes 'gurgle' when you hit it with a heavy book: Don't hit it with a heavy book.

Transistor radio in cornflakes: Remove radio from cornflakes. (This should be done before adding milk.)

The history of POP

PART TWO

Pop music is a fusion of negro blues and the Eurovision song contest. This was Cliff Richard's idea.

No other television-based European song competition can be said to have influenced pop music as much as the Eurovision song contest has. This is how it happened.

After Lincoln freed the slaves, Cliff was at a loose end. Sure, he'd invented the blues, and the spirituals, and scored a personal triumph singing 'Old Man River' in *Showboat*, but he still hadn't invented pop music, and that was what he really wanted to do. 'There must be something else' he used to think to himself rhythmically.

One night, Cliff was in bed with Una Stubbs, wishing she was Sue Barker, and Cliff said 'Get off it Una! I'd rather have a game of charades.' It was from this chance comment that 'Give Us a Clue' was born. Not many people know this, but besides inventing pop music, Cliff Richard invented Lionel Blair.

Back in England and bored with writing all Elvis' hits, Cliff took Una to Liverpool on a whim, (actually, it was a train brilliant!). By this time Una was practising her tennis for many hours a day and calling herself Sue. 'You'd do anything to get a look at my nob, wouldn't you' said Cliff as they alighted at Lime Street station. 'Yes' said Una.

That day was the most important day in history. Cliff stood in the crowded sweaty underground club watching four raw, leather clad, gangly youths on stage who had a sort of magic all of their own. 'I only came in for a piss,' said Cliff to Brian Epstein who was standing beside him nursing the most phenomenal erection in the history of rock and roll, 'but now I've had the most fantastic idea.' And he had, for as he stood, there, in the Cavern Club, in 1962, watching an unknown band called the Beatles, Cliff had a vision of a satellite television link-up whereby every country in Europe could submit a song to be judged by an international panel of jurors, for a two-hour special, with the Lionel Blair dancers filling in the gaps, 'That's it,' he cried, 'the Eurovision Song Contest.' 'Piss off,' said Brian, 'I'm trying to discover the Beatles.'

And that's how it all happened.

the new kama sutra

1 **Foreplay.**

4 **The James Dean.**

5 **The Naughty Hoover.**

9 **Born to be wild.**

8 **The Gene Kelly.**

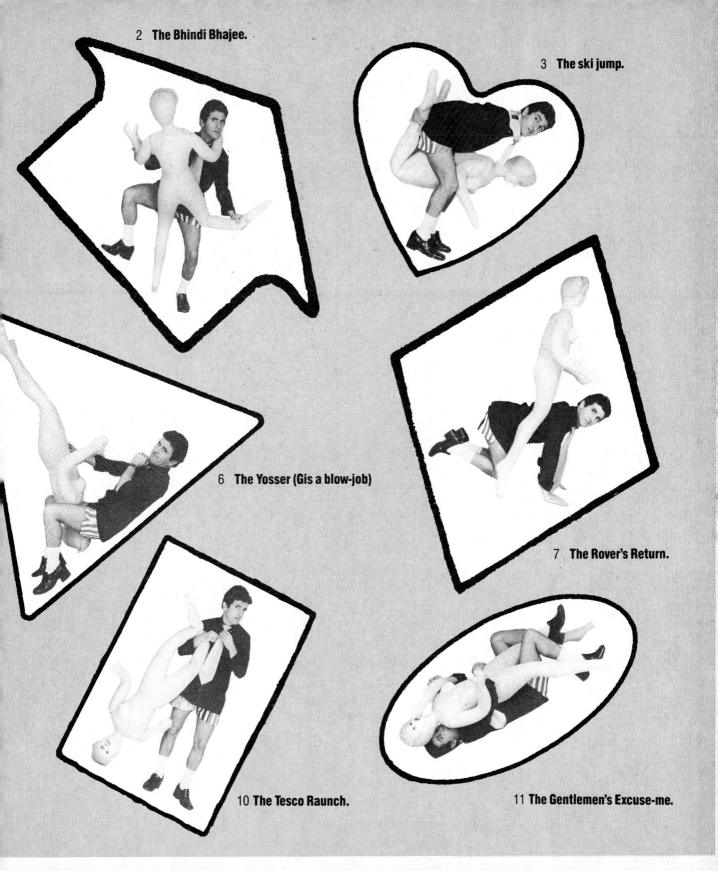

2 **The Bhindi Bhajee.**

3 **The ski jump.**

6 **The Yosser (Gis a blow-job)**

7 **The Rover's Return.**

10 **The Tesco Raunch.**

11 **The Gentlemen's Excuse-me.**

EDUCACION

● *How to cheat at exams*

Anarchists do not swot for exams.

In fact, anarchists don't do exams at all.

But if for some extra special reason, an anarchist does have to do an exam (like being made to by his or her mum) ANARCHISTS CHEAT.

METHOD ONE

Write all the answers out on your thigh, and when teach isn't looking, have a quick peek. *IMPORTANT.* This technique only really works if you are in a dress. I mean not me, of course – girlies. I wouldn't wear a blue and white gingham frock with a fabulous pink satin belt that you can get for only – er, anyway over to you, Mike.

METHOD TWO

Hi, Mike the cool person here, passing an exam is like passing water – it's a piece of piss. One method to avoid is the old 'Write it on a piece of chewing gum and when Miss comes, eat it method'. It takes approximately six thousand sticks of gum to accommodate the average essay. If you really fancy this method why not use pancakes or popadoms? Pizzas are good too, but remember, you can only write on one side of a pizza.

METHOD THREE

Rick here with an absolutely brilliant idea! I'm afraid it's only any good for boys so girlies will have to use Mike's pizza method I'm afraid. My idea is amazingly graet and foolproof, and here it is.

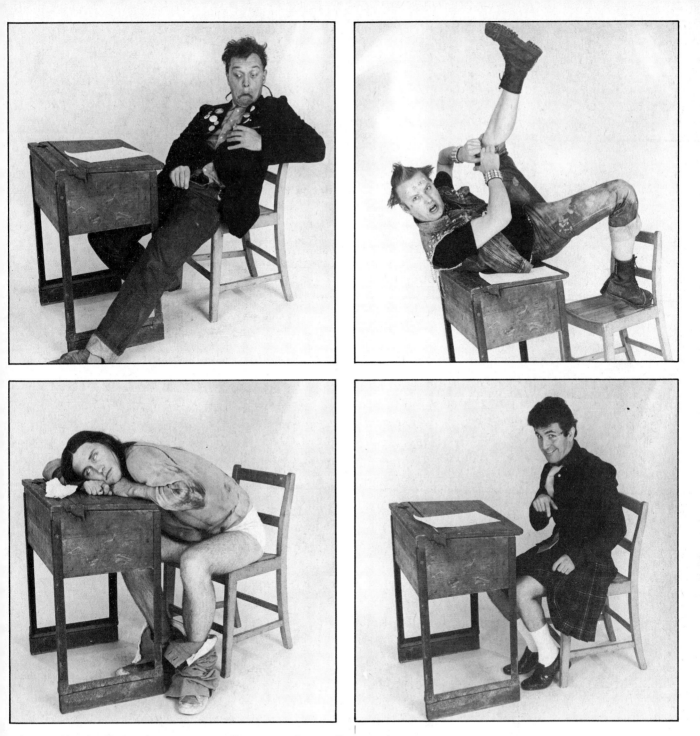

The night before the exam, when you're at home in your room, think dirty. Yes, that's right, *think dirty*. Bet you never thought passing exams could be so much fun, right guys! Now, not a lot of people know this, but when boys

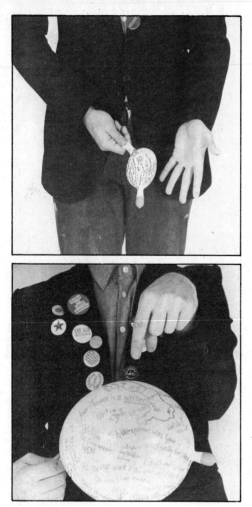

'think dirty' their thingys go all big and hard. Yes, bet tha surprised a lot of you. Anyway, when it's got just about a big as you think it's going to get (and only you can be th judge of that), grab your biro, and quickly write all you swotty cheat stuff onto the nob.

A bit later on, when all the excitement is over, your 'thingy will have returned to normal, and you will see that th writing has almost completely disappeared! Leaving th appearance of only a few prominent blue veins, or perhap a surrealistic tattoo.

The next day, make sure you go into the exam with no panties on. Then, when the going gets tough, and you need help, gently unzip your flies, and start 'thinking dirty'. Like magic, the answers will rise up and appear before your very eyes (well, before your very tummy button) as if from nowhere. If then, you see teach' approach, you will be gripped with fear, and without you even trying, everything will collapse, and the answers will completely disappear. BRILLIANT!

N.B. I said earlier that this idea was of no use to girls, but of course with a bit of co-operation, it can be. Remember guys, this could be the only time in your lives when you hear a girly say, 'Can I see your nob?'.

M E T H O D   F O U R

My idea is better than owning your own chainsaw, and even a nerdy like Rick could do it. What you do is, for a few weeks before the exam, every now and then you have to say, 'Oh lordy lordy, deary me, I think I'm going deaf', and when a teach' says, 'What's the capital of France?' you say, 'really? I prefer elephants'. By this method, people will slowly believe you to be deaf. Then one day, you start wearing a 'hearing aid' but it is not really a hearing aid, really it's a

Sony Walkman. Into this 'hearing aid' on the day of the exam, you can submit a carefully prepared tape of all the answers. BRILLIANT.

NB It is *very* important not to mix up your tapes.

SCUMBAG COLLEGE EXAM.

MEDICINE. (main subject)

NAME VYVYAN

Describe how the over-use of antibiotics has led to the emergence of the 'super virus'

IF YOU LIKE TO GAMBLE
BABY I'M YOUR MAN
YOU WIN SOME LOSE SOME
ITS ALL THE SAMETOME THE ACE OF SPADES
THE ACE OF SPADES

THE ACE OF SPADES
THE ACE OF SPADES
THATS THE WAY I LIKE IT BABY

I DON'T WANT TO
LIVE
FOREVER

SCUMBAG COLLEGE EXAM.

CURRENT AFFAIRS. (subsidiary subject)

NAME VYVYAN

Discuss events leading up to Edward Heath's decision to hold a referendum on whether Britain should join the EEC.

NEEEEAAAAAGHH
I SAW THE FRIEND
OF THE DEVILS DAUGHTERS
SISTER

AAAGH!
AAAA-AAAGH!
NIGHTMARE OF DOOM
AND MOTORBIKE
FRENZY

M E T H O D   F I V E

Well, like, I go along with Mike's pizza method, except I would use only *one lentil*.

Yes I would carry only one lentil's worth of information into that exam. Because I have been inside my head, and on that journey, I asked myself, 'Oh Neil, how much information can be got onto one lentil?' and my head replied, 'All the information in the world Neil, if need be.'

And I pondered this long. Considering the camel and the eye of the needle, and the angels on the head of a pin, and finally I say the great truth that this idea implied. 'It would have to be a fucking big lentil,' I said, and my head replied to me, 'Yes, it would.'

So like, anyway, that's what I'd do. I'd grow an enormous lentil, and write everything I needed onto it and take it into the exam, and cheat. And if I saw the teacher coming, I'd soak it in water for a night, boil it, and eat it.

20 foolproof excuses for not doing an essay

1 What essay?

2 I did it, but I accidentally tore it up

3 I haven't got any hands

4 I'm dead

5 A burglar took it

6 The *Times Literary Supplement* wanted to see it first

7 Up yours, four-eyes

8 We're too poor to afford toilet paper and my father has dysentery

9 I was in a plane crash and we had to eat each other's essays

10 The police confiscated it

11 I know it all – what's the point in writing it down?

12 My desk caught fire

13 I'm undergoing a personality crisis

14 I posted it to you – didn't you get it? – huh, the Post Office these days, I don't know

15 I made this bookmark instead

16 Everyone says you're pregnant so I didn't think you'd be here today

17 You must be mad – you've already marked it and given it back to me – I got an A

18 Look, just get off my back, will you?

19 Oh God, I think I'm going to be sick all over you

20 Did you say you wanted me to take all my clothes off?

● 8 foolproof ways to get a detention

1 Go up to the detention list and add your name at the bottom.

2 During French, while the teacher isn't looking, sneak up to the blackboard and write, 'All French teachers are wankers' on it, then sneak back to your desk. Then, when the master discovers it and asks who did it, put your hand up and say, 'I did, sir.'

3 Go up to any games teacher and ask them the time. Games teachers are notoriously stupid and hate being caught out like this.

4 Go up to the headmaster at morning assembly, get your undercarriage out and say, 'Look what's for breakfast, sir.'

5 Claim to be a famous pop star of your choice and refuse to come to school unless you have a limo from your house and a dressing room full of fags, booze, drugs, etc and roadies crawling under your desk during lessons.

6 Phone the headmaster's wife, give your name, claim you're running an escort agency from the school library, and say that her husband is one of your most regular clients and that if you don't get £50,000 in used notes by morning break the next day, then you're going to the Sunday Papers. (NB: If you get the cash you can buy a detention – everyone knows how corrupt prefects are.)

7 Sneak up behind the most frightening Maths master you can find and make a sudden farty sound. Then shout, 'Crikey, what a belter! What did you have for lunch, sir?' Then when he casually turns round and says, 'All right insect, fifty lines – I must not make it look as if the Maths master's dropped one,' say, 'Pardon sir?' and he'll lose his temper and shout 'FIFTY LINES!!' Then, really fast, draw something like this:

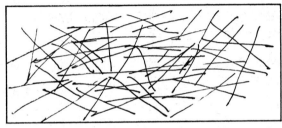

. . . then hand it to him holding your nose and saying, 'Here you are wiffy – fifty lines.' The detention is a cert.

8 Before the school swimming gala, go to the local fish shop and buy a bucketful of crabs. When the great day arrives sneak up behind the Deputy Head before he makes his speech and put them under his chair. Then, when he gets up to speak, leap up and shout, 'Look out everyone – the Deputy Head's got crabs!' He'll grab his nasties and go red and at that point say, 'No sir, under your chair'; then, when he says, 'Thank you my boy, thank you. I could have been in for a nasty shock there, I must reward you, is there anything you would like?', say 'Yes sir, could I have a detention please?'

exchange visits

Exchange visits are completely bloody crap and must be avoided at all costs. Only wankers that have pencil cases shaped like bananas and space shuttles and day-glo pencils with miniature trolls with blue hair and a huge hole between the legs shoved on the end and sticky labels saying, 'Please Return this V.I.P.C. – very important pencil case – to Geoff Utter-Spazmo Form VB actually choose to go on exchange visits. In most cases, however, an exchange visit is organised by a teacher or a parent who claims that it is FOR YOUR OWN GOOD*. As soon as you get wind of any such goings-on it is important to take immediate evasive action.

PLAN A: *EVASIVE ACTION*
These are some of the things you can do:

(But this is)

1 Leave home
2 Kill parents/teacher
3 Kill yourself
4 Start a war with the country you are destined for
5 Eat twelve bars of Exlax the day before you are due to leave.

Even the best laid plans of mice and men can get ripped up into little pieces thrown up over and flushed down the U-bend. If all attempts to stop this revolting excursion fail and you find yourself puking up on the Sealink to Boulogne (exchange visits are almost always to Froggie-land – anywhere else and you're either a bloody little swot doing an optional second language and deserve everything you get) it is now time to put plan B into effect.

* *This is a lie. As is everything teachers say.*

PLAN B: *GET SENT HOME IMMEDIATELY*

Methods:

a Burn your exchange house down. (The French for buying a flame-thrower i
'Donnez-moi un jeteur de flamme!).

b Pretend to be German. Shout 'Achtung spitfire!' a lot and strut around the town
square looking haughty.

c Assassinate M. le Mayor or any leading local politician.

d Get old very quickly, make a lot of money, learn to fly, buy a plane, bomb the
house.

e Eat fifty bars of Ex-lax on arrival.

PLAN C: *FIGHTING BACK*

As everyone knows, the worst thing about a foreign exchange is the foreigner. The
exchange is no ordinary foreigner either – you can't kick sand in his face and
shout, 'Get out of it, frogs-legs, what did you do in the war?', you can't stick pins in
his lilo when he's half a mile from shore and can't swim very well . . . and why not
Well, for a start, you're unlikely to be anywhere near a beach, and secondly and
most sinister and revolting of all, because you are ALONE. ALONE with THE
ENEMY.

The ENEMY's name will be either Marcel, Michel or Jean-Marie. He wil
almost certainly be carrying a flick-knife and has no qualms about inflicting
physical damage to your person – don't forget, not only does he speak good
French which you can't and won't (ref. 'I'm a death rider from Hell, and I don't go
to French lessons' Motorhead '82) but he's also VERY VERY GOOD AT CRYING.
In froggie terms, crying is the signal for six or seven older brothers of whose
existence you have been previously unaware, to leap out of the woodwork, and
beat the shit out of you.

All this vilence sounds like fun but it's not. You are alone, remember, and it
happens behind closed doors. The parents never find out, and you can't complain
because they speak the same bloody language as the others.

REMEMBER – DON'T EVER EVER EVER EVER EVER EVER EVER EVER
EVER EVER GO ON AN EXCHANGE.

NOW YOUR ENEMY

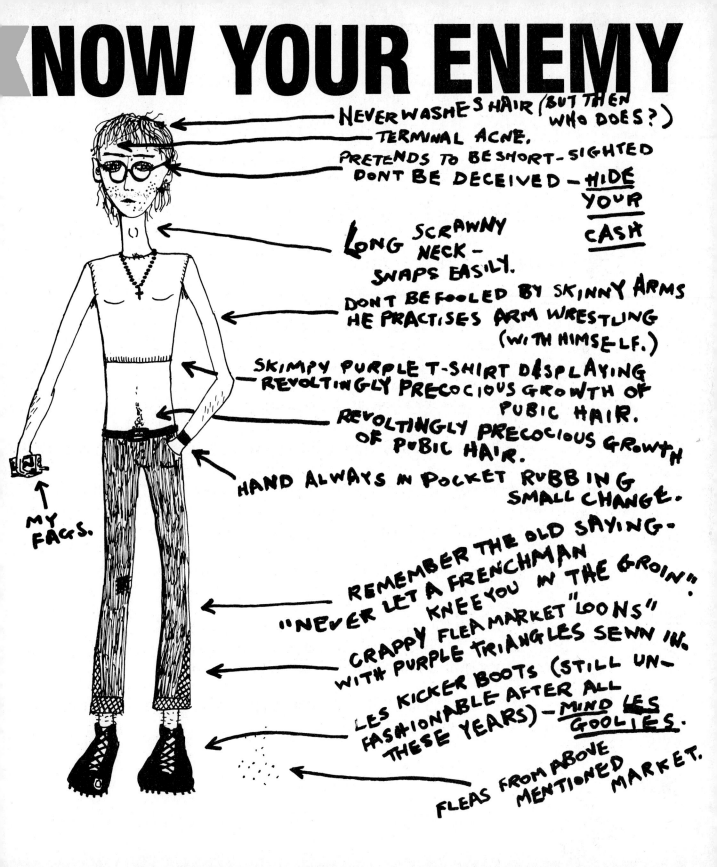

NEVER WASHES HAIR (BUT THEN WHO DOES?)

TERMINAL ACNE.

PRETENDS TO BE SHORT-SIGHTED
DONT BE DECEIVED — HIDE YOUR CASH

LONG SCRAWNY NECK —
SNAPS EASILY.

DONT BE FOOLED BY SKINNY ARMS
HE PRACTISES ARM WRESTLING
(WITH HIMSELF.)

SKIMPY PURPLE T-SHIRT DISPLAYING
REVOLTINGLY PRECOCIOUS GROWTH OF
PUBIC HAIR.

REVOLTINGLY PRECOCIOUS GROWTH
OF PUBIC HAIR.

HAND ALWAYS IN POCKET RUBBING
SMALL CHANGE.

REMEMBER THE OLD SAYING —
"NEVER LET A FRENCHMAN
KNEE YOU IN THE GROIN."

CRAPPY FLEA MARKET "LOONS"
WITH PURPLE TRIANGLES SEWN IN.

LES KICKER BOOTS (STILL UN-
FASHIONABLE AFTER ALL
THESE YEARS) — MIND LES
GOOLIES.

FLEAS FROM ABOVE
MENTIONED MARKET.

MY FAGS.

TOTAL THEATRE

by Rick

Theatre doesn't always have to be boring like *Hamlet* and *Starlight Express*. No. Theatre can be now and great. Theatre can be for you and me. And you don't even need an Arts Council grant. It's true.

This is a play we did at school. I wrote it and everyone said it was Reeeeeelly Grate. We did it for the old people and all in the Lower Fourth. Miss Kershaw liked it a lot and said I was the best: I agreed with her.

THE TEENAGERS   *by Rick*

CAST
JUMBO: ....*Martin Thomson*
KEITH: ....*Timmy Dashwood*
SPIDER: ....*Rick*

SCENE: A CANAL BANK

JUMBO: Oh what a lovely canal and I'm not talking about your anal passage I'm sorry Keith and Spider I know that was a tasteless joke and not at all funny.

SPIDER: Who cares whether it was funny or not? I want a fag. I mean that's what I came down here for so who's got the cigarettes? Come on cough up.

KEITH: That's exactly what you will be doing if you smoke fags Spider – coughing up.

SPIDER: Don't make me laugh Keith – I know you you're as bad as Liverpool.

KEITH: What do you mean Spider?

SPIDER: Well, when you're in Liverpool and you ask someone for a fag they're all too busy up the football* to give you one.

KEITH: But Liverpool is the greatest football team in the world and you won't catch any of them smoking fags, even though they're old enough to smoke. You wouldn't catch Kevin Keegan with a fag Spider.

JUMBO: Kevin Keegan doesn't play for Liverpool. Anyway, he is a fashion model so don't bring him into this argument. I wish I could live on a canal boat – it would be so peaceful sitting in locks.

SPIDER: Locks locks locks is that all you can speak about – imprisonment? You worry me you know Jumbo. One of these days you're going to freak out, and then you'll really freak out.

KEITH: Yes Jumbo you really are a head case why don't you see a psychoanalyst?

SPIDER: Because he's not mad Keith, he's just like one of us always searching for something, that elusive something so elusive that it's hard to find.

KEITH: Yes I suppose you're right Spider. You've got your fags and Jumbo's got his locks, I've got a verucca so we've all got problems.

JUMBO: Hey look at those girls (POINTING). Just looking at them makes me want to have it off with them.

KEITH: I don't believe I'm hearing this don't be so pathetic about women Jumbo. When you shout like that it shows that all you really want is to have sex with them.

SPIDER: Look out everybody – Nuclear War!

T H E   E N D

One of the graet things about life is feet, and one of the graet things about feet is that they're graet for having Cheezey Feet Contests. All you need is everyone in your house, an enclosed space and your feet. Everyone gets into the cupboard and on the command 'Cheese it you Rebels!' takes off their shoes and tries to get their feet as near to their opponents' noses as possible. The first one out of the cupboard has to eat all the other guys' socks.

Adolescent Depression

When I was a teenager, right, I was only seriously depressed like twice—once for four years, and once for five. The first of these periods hit me when I hit thirteen. This depression followed hard on the one I'd been having when I was twelve, which like dated back to a bad vibe I had as a foetus, but those were childhood depressions, which are not like what I'm talking about right now.

OK so this first adolescent depression resulted in a sudden realisation that **everything** in the world was

TOTALLY AND UTTERLY BUM.

I was sitting in my room, right, and my parents had gone out in the car, and I suddenly thought, 'Wow, supposing they crash and die, what will I do without their money'. It was then that I realised the world's greatest truth,

ONE BUM VIBE LEADS TO ANOTHER.

This is true, and will be true for all time. So, right, you only need to have one bad vibe right, like early on, and you will never escape. My bum vibe was being born, it all went down hill from there.

'Because of the blunt stylus, the album was ruined.
Because we threw away the album, the joint wasn't rolled on it.
Because we hadn't smoked the stash, the pigs found it the next day.
Because the pigs found it, we got busted and fined.
Because of the fine, we like blew out our grants.
Because we were breadless, we couldn't buy a new stylus.
Because of the blunt stylus, the album was ruined . . .'

YOU CAN'T BEAT THE SYSTEM, THEY'LL GET YOU EVERY TIME, THE BASTARDS, RIGHT?

Between my first and second adolescent depressions,

I WAS HAPPY FOR EIGHT MINUTES!!!

Yeah, I was fifteen and a half and this is how it happened. I *discovered drugs*. I tuned up, freaked in, and dropped around. I found God and happiness within myself, I like knew, and saw, THE WHOLE TRUTH, and it was a trip man, a real trip.

This is how it happened. Me and my like groove pal, Rollock, were in Leamington Spa, just sort of digging the summer and drawing on our jeans in biro . . . when this guy I knew from school, well, he was my best mate actually, came up and said, 'Hey, Neil and Rollock, d'you wanna score some *acid*?'

FREAK OUT!!! DID WE? HAVE I GOT LONG HAIR?

So like we scored a couple of tabs . . . and *dropped them* (which is groove talk for eating them). Like 50p a tab, and it was done. My very first electric cool laid acid trip . . .

Instantly my previous adolescent depression fell away from me, like Gandalf casting aside his old grey cloak, my head seemed to detach itself and float above me, I looked down and I could see that my nob was bigger than Heathrow airport. Then this like space ship landed on it, and Jimi Hendrix got out and started playing 'Electric Ladyland' on a harp made out of my pubes, except it wasn't Jimi, it was JESUS! and he said, 'watch the sunshine dance Neil, there are no more bum vibes,' and I said 'each one of my thoughts is a glittering bubble, floating in space for all eternity,' and then there was this incredibly groovy dancing flower in front of me, and it looked a bit like Rollock, and it was singing, and the song it sang was . . .

'This is an orange tictac man! we've been ripped off,' and that was when my second adolescent depression started.

RICK THINKS NEIL IS RIGHT SHOCKER!!!

Much as I loathe him I must admit that Neil is right about feeling low, all kids get it, it's part of being angry, and Cliff Richard invented a name for it, it's called 'the blues'.

The birth of the blues

Spots
Girlies, (or boys if you are a girly)
Mums
Unfashionable trousers
International capitalism

The first way to beat the blues is to write a poem. I wrote this one, and it's brilliant, and it helped me a lot. So that's my advice to you. If you're feeling depressed, read my poem.

RICK'S TEEN ANGUISH POEM

oh god,
why
am I so much more sensitive than everybody else?
why
do I feel things so much more acutely than them,
and understand so much more.
I bet I'm the first person who's ever felt as rotten
   as this.
could it be
that I'm going to grow up
to be a great poet and thinker, and all those other
   wankers in my class are going to have to work
   in factories or go on the dole?
yes, I think it could.

VYVYAN SPEAKS: *Depression? piss off.*

Yes, very clever I'm sure Vyvyan, try telling that to Vincent Van Gogh, but he won't listen, and why? Because he cut his ear off, and why? Because he was depressed.

● Adolescent Depression

Why was Van Gogh so depressed? there are three reasons.

1 His girly didn't like him.
2 His parents kept hassling him to tidy his room.
3 Don Maclean's song.

1 What to do if your girly doesn't like you

a Abuse yourself in the lavatory. Not a bad solution this, however it is no substitute for intellectual conversation, unless you are a ventriloquist, in which case, you can chat to your nob.

b Say to yourself 'Love, who needs it, I'm a wild eyed loner, standing at the gates of oblivion, I'll get drunk and write poetry, I don't need friends, I have my genius, when I've drunk myself to death and left a sick stained masterpiece behind me, they'll be sorry', then have a half of cider and write a teen anguish poem.

ON NO ACCOUNT CUT OFF YOUR EAR.

2 What to do if your mum keeps hassling you to tidy your room

a Go into an unbelievable enormous *sulk*. Say loads of things like, 'I've got to be allowed to be myself mum, you don't understand me or my music',

b Tell her to piss off (this was Vyvyan's idea)

c ON NO ACCOUNT CUT OFF YOUR EAR

3 What to do if Don Maclean writes a soppy nob end song about you

a Cut off your ears.

● *REMEMBER DEPRESSION, LIKE HAVING WILLY BATTLES IN THE SHOWERS, IS PART OF GROWING UP.*

ade the tea?

● **Here's another problem for you, readers.**

CHAPTER V *A typical morning*

The sound of the telephone's insistent ringing woke Rick that morning. He stretched casually, his sturdy muscular arms and fine body pressing masculinely, but not in an overaggressively dominant way, against the fine fabric of his mint-green polyester pyjamas which had been a present from a grateful female associate. His chiselled face with its raunchy skin-tone which always drove women wild was marred, but only slightly, by the red-rimmed tired eyes of ice-blue, which everyone agreed were one of his best features. It seemed like only seven or eight hours since he had tumbled into bed after the previous night's amazing bash at the élite Revolutionary Poetsoc do. 'Yes, we Anarchists are a pretty PROPERTY SCUMBAG COLLEGE hard-living, fast-drinking bunch of people,' he thought to himself. 'It must have been after midnight when we left the Union Bar.' His quiet musings were rudely interrupted by a knock at the door. 'What do you want?' he growled. 'Telephone,' murmured a rather weedy and pathetic voice, its owner obviously too overawed by Rick's extraordinary presence to dare enter the room. 'Rings a bell!' Rick quipped, his mind as always, working at lightning speed. There was no reply. 'Never mind,' said Rick kindly, 'I'll explain it to you later.'

He sprang on muscles of coiled steel from the hard couch of repose. His senses felt curiously sharp that morning, and there NOW WASH YOUR HANDS was a strange, but not unpleasant, tingling in his loins. However there was no time for that now. He flung on his tartan smoking jacket and strode out into the hallway, noticing briefly that some long-haired half-wit must have been standing very near his door. He stepped over the prone, effeminate figure and strode towards the top of the stairs.

His razor-sharp eyes spotted the danger – but too late. An evil, juvenile fascist had set a trap for the Man of

T h e
H o u s e
N o v e l

Destiny. His whole life seemed to flash before Rick as he tumbled head-first down the hard wooden stairs–the Russian countess who had chosen to exile herself rather than risk not winning his love, the famous film star who had sent him a signed photograph in the hope that he PROPERTY SCUMBAG COLLEGE would keep it under the floorboards next to his bed, the wild and beautiful student who concealed her consuming passion under a mock exterior of scorn. Was this the end of the man who no woman could resist? . . .

CHAPTER VI Rick Escapes and Saves the Universe

Slowly Rick regained consciousness. At first there was only a vague sensation of movement, then a sharper one of pain. But Rick was no stranger to that. A rebel-man eats pain for breakfast–especially when he's in France–and Rick was one of the hardest, spikiest-haired, smoothest-talking, no-prisoner-takingest he-men in the rebel business. He could handle it–just as soon as he got his hands untied–NOW WASH YOUR HANDS. But suddenly Rick died and nobody cared because he was such a complete bastard and a girly weed. The man responsible for his demise, Herr Generalissimo Steppenführer Vyvyan Basterd VC, DC, VIP, BA stepped back from the already rotting corpse and laughed. So did everybody else because they were afraid of what their commander would do if they didn't. He was a man capable of conquering the world–he just hadn't bothered yet that's all. 'Big Vyv' they called him, because he was. Not only was he hung like a Bramah bull but he could do forty-eight press-ups in a row and slam his balls in the fridge door without so much as wincing. One day this incredible man would be a doctor–he would PROPERTY SCUMBAG COLLEGE take the Hypocritical Oath and earn loads and loads of money to buy lager and fags with, but at the moment he lived for today and got his kicks where he could: heavy metal music, fast cars, extreme vilence and Rick's bollocks. Field Marshal Vyvyan Basterd cast his eyes over his battleship. Then he picked them up again and replaced one of them in its socket. As far as the eye could see men in uniforms hurried about their business – loading big guns, refuelling the private fleet of Stukas and Harrier jump-jets, arming nuclear warheads – anything to keep in their leader's good books and stop him kicking their teeth in. 'What shall I blow up today?' wondered Admiral Vyv. 'Canada perhaps, or maybe Japan? Oh God – it's no use, I'm NOW WASH YOUR HANDS completely bloody bored with the whole thing – I'll just have to set Neil's bed on fire that's all.'

CHAPTER VII
Something Really Heavy Happens

It was really heavy. Really really really really really heavy. And not just really really really really really heavy, but HEAVY. H.E.A.V.Y. The most negative vibe in Vibesville, the lead vocalist of bummers, the King Crimson of the Hassle Brigade. It was too heavy for words. It certainly was. 'Ooh Mike,' she moaned in ecstasy. 'Your chopper is so heavy it takes three of us glamorous models to lift it.' Mike turned PROPERTY SCUMBAG COLLEGE over in bed bringing a sigh of awe to the chick's lips. 'Well it's lucky I've got sixteen of you then,' he said casually. 'Who's next?' There was total silence. 'I-I-I'm sorry Mike,' stammered Samantha, a tall beautiful blonde calendar girl who was completely nude, 'it's just that you're such a hunk of manhood that you've worn us all out.' Mike kept his cool. 'So what do I do now?' he smiled wryly. Samantha turned her green dove-like eyes towards him and breathed softly NOW WASH YOUR HANDS.

CHAPTER VIII *Even Heavier*

Meanwhile Neil went to the toilet again. He was always ill and suffering but he was very brave and never complained even though he had to go the toilet ten times as much as the other guys in his house because he had this Indian dysentery thing and often oh no some fascist has used the last bit of pape. . .

LEON TROTSKY'S

Just fancy that !

Dear Leon,
'A lot of strange things seem to be happening at the moment. Last week I put my rubbish out on Thursday evening and it was collected on Friday as usual. But my friend Gordon who lives in Birkenhead put his rubbish out on the same night and it wasn't collected till *Monday*. When he rang up the council to complain they told him the collection day had been changed from *Friday* to *Monday* – so this week I put my rubbish out on *Sunday* night as did my friend Gordon. They collected *his* rubbish on *Monday* but mine sat there till *Friday* and when I rang up the council to complain they told me the collection day was *Friday*. Ain't it amazin'?!!

Yours
Mr James Buchanan, Gosforth

Leon says: Spooky, eh?

And Mrs Anita Prior has sent us this photo of a sign in Kettering.

Leon says: **Let's hope dogs don't learn to read, eh readers?**

★ ★ ★ ★
★ **W E I R D**
B U T
★ **T R U E** ★
The fattest man in the world was Senor Miguel Disraeli of Guadalahara. He was so fat that his wife suggested he go on a diet.
★ ★ ★ ★

Literary criticism, the analysis of a Cliff Richard lyric

Power to all our friends by Cliff (Eurovision song contest 1973)

By which I doubt he means Vyvyan, Mike or Neil

Power to all our friends
To the music that never ends.

He must have heard Neil's Genesis LP's

To the people we want to be
Baby power to you and me.

Think he's referring to me in this sentence.

he's talking to you kids, aren't you proud?

CHORUS

Bloody raunchy stuff eh?

Power to the boys who play Rock and Roll,
And made my life so sweet.

Well you've made our lives sweet Cliff, so power to you kids!)

And to the girls I knew before,
And those I've yet to meet.

Who bloody said Cliff was gay! (not that it matters)

REPEAT VERSE
MAN OF FEW WORDS

whatch out Sue! the old dog's still got a roving eye, you can't tame Cliff!

And bloody right, it's well worth repeating, I'd said "repeat verse 10 times"

Congratulations by Cliff (Eurovision song contest, 1968)

Congratulations, and celebrations,
I want the world to know that I'm in love with you.
Congratulations and jubilations.
I want the world to know that I'm in love with you.

WHAT MORE CAN WE SAY CLIFF, BUT "CONGRATULATIONS" TO YOU FOR FORTY FIVE YEARS AT THE TOP OF THE POPS!

⊕ health and efficiency

● THERE IS NOTHING WRONG WITH SPOTS!! *by Vyvyan*

What oh what is at the heart of this concerted media campaign against acne? There is nothing wrong with acne, in fact, acne is great. Bloody hell, if I see just one more of those 'Spotjuice works on the zit in three different, biological ways' commercials, I'll eat the telly and poo it into a Magimix! Bloody bloody bloody bloody! everyone goes on about how incredibly great it is to be so young, and they make nerdy div films like 'Grease 2' ('Grease Poo' I call it) and then they try to turn you into a leper if you've got a spot on your bot!

When you go down the puberty, your balls drop, or your tits grow, and you **get spotty**! They don't try and sell you ball removing cream or tit disguising cosmetics, **SO WHY PICK ON SPOTS**???

I DECLARE THIS INTERNATIONAL YEAR OF THE SPOT. DON'T BE INTIMIDATED– WEAR YOUR SPOTS WITH PRIDE!

A word from Rick

Does Mrs Thatcher have spots? Did Adolf Hitler have spots? No! And why? Because they're square, they're boring, they're grown ups, and they're Nazi's.

KIDS HAVE SPOTS, AND KIDS ARE GREAT!

Grown-ups are scared of spots. Spots mean pop music, spots mean having fun, all the things they're too square to understand. When a grown-up sees a great big spot coming down the street towards them, boy! Freak out! 'Street fight' they think, 'West Side Story', 'switch blades, motor bikes, teen mania'. They sneer at 'acne' because they want you to be like them.

BUYING CLEARASAL IS JUST ONE MORE WAY OF VOTING CONSERVATIVE

Che Guevara was spotty. So was Martin Luther King. Lenin had a great big one right on his nose, and two on the corner of his lip, and as for Trotsky, well 'Trot the spot' as the commissars used to call him had a face like rhubarb and custard.

All great people have a few spots every now and then.

PEOPLE WHO ADMIT TO GETTING A SPOT EVERY NOW AND THEN	PEOPLE WHO PRETEND THEY NEVER GET SPOTS
Cliff Richard	Thatcher
Neil Kinnock	Stalin
Felicity Kendall	Genghis Khan

Vyvyan of the TV's famous 'Robin's Nest' says *'Have you ever woken up to find that you've only got a tiny little spot and you're scared your friends won't notice it? Well, with new CLEARASDAY you don't have to worry any more.*

'The magic pen'

No-one can miss it now!

Vyvyan 'before' with a barely noticeable spot on his upper lip

Popular myths exposed by our medical correspondent

Roughage makes you poo.

Let us scotch this myth and give credit where credit is due. Bottoms do all the work, they should get the credit. After all, bottoms don't claim to taste nice in a bowl with milk and sugar, so why should All Bran get away with claiming that it can poo?

THE VYVYAN 'L&C' DIET

Breakfast: A bowl of curry and a pint of lager, or lager and lime, no milk or sugar.

Elevenses: Just one or two onion bhajis if you're peckish.

Lunch:: A curry and a few pints of lager. No dessert.

Tea: A bag of samosas from the take-away, and a can of lager. Avoid nibblin at biscuits and sweet things, if you're still not full, have a couple of stuffed nans and some more lager.

Supper: A huge curry and loads of lager followed by black coffee—but no cream, naughty!

Last thing: Avoid anything too heavy, perhaps a tikka or tandoori, washed down with lager. Hot lager with a big teaspoonful of Ovaltine is revolting.

THE VYVYAN 'L & C' CRASH DIET

How to lose at least a couple of stone, in *twelve hours or less!*

Go out for the evening and eat the most enormous curry you could possibly imagine, and drink so much lager that you think you're going to burst. Then get a cab home and weigh yourself. Then go to bed, having first opened the window. The next morning, after you have been to the lavatory, weigh yourself again. The difference in the two weights will be astounding.

NEIL'S HANDY RECIPES

A lot of people faced with the idea of me doing a cookery book, might say 'Oh God, total and complete bummer, it'll be really boring, because it'll be nothing but lentil recipes. Nothing could be further from the truth, lentil recipes are very interesting'. Here are a few of my faves.

LENTILS AND CHEESE:

ingredients: *lentils and cheese.*

method: *get together some lentils and cheese.*

LENTILS ON TOAST:

ingredients: *lentils and bread (not money).*

method: *put bread under hot grill until it is brown. Take bread out, turn it over and put it back. When both sides are brown, remove from grill and sprinkle lentils on top.*

LENTILS:

ingredients: *lentils.*

method: *put in mouth, chew and swallow.*

LENTILS À LA DUCK À L'ORANGE:

ingredients: *lentils and a French restaurant.*

method: *take some lentils and go to the restaurant. Order some Duck À L'Orange, and when it arrives, put the lentils on the plate as well.*

LENTIL SURPRISE:

any dish that does not contain lentils.

LENTIL SICK: INGREDIENTS - LENTILS AND FINGERS
METHOD - EAT THE LENTILS AND STICK
YOUR FINGERS DOWN YOUR THROAT. NV.

Advanced Cookery Course:

DEVILLED MOTORBIKE CHAIN

(Serves 10)

Ingredients
3 litres oil (multigrade)
1 bottle vodka
5 cups ordinary gravel
salt and pepper
1 motorbike chain

Method

1 Place chain, oil, gravel in large mixing bowl. Season to taste.

4 Add Vodka.

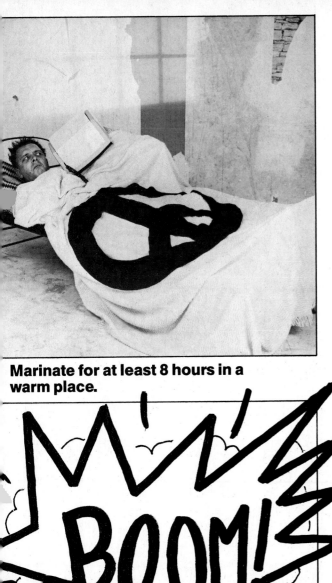

Marinate for at least 8 hours in a warm place.

3 ■ **Transfer mixture into saucepan.**

BOOM!

Insert lighted match.

6 ■ **Serve warm with optional plaster garnish – makes an ideal winter picnic.**

the Яussian Яevolution

SCENE ONE:

(This is a play about a socialist revolution so we start with Scene One. If it was about an anarchist revolution, we'd probably start on Scene Twelve of a totally different play! And then when our mateys said, 'Hi anarchists, are you doing a play?', we'd say 'No, we're playing football, so stick that up your Kronstat Thatcher!' But anyway, it's a socialist play, so here goes with Scene One.

SCENE ONE

Russia. Just a bit of it, not the whole thing, thank you very much. A small bit of Russia, in fact, the bit just inside the Winter Palace. It is a sumptuous ballroom (oh yes ha ha Vyvyan, no it's not a room where you keep your balls). You can easily create a theatrical impression of sumptuous extravagance with string, glue, and mum's baco-foil.

ENTER THE TSAR AND SOME EVIL CRONIES, COUNT BASTARDSKY, COUNT GIRLYKOV, AND COUNT TOTALANDUTTERNOBEND-FARTYBREATHSKY.

TSAR:

Ha ha ha, I feel like a complete bastard today.

COUNT GIRLYKOV:

Fair enough, I'll go and get Rasputin.

ALL:

(SING AND DANCE) Ra Ra Rasputeeen.
            Russia's favourite love machine.   *(Copyright Boney M 1977)*

ENTER COUNT GIRLYKOV WITH RASPUTIN, DOING UP HIS TROUSERS.

RASPUTIN:

Lock up your daughters, Mr Sexy Peasant's in town.

TSAR:

Shut up hippy I've had it up to here with you.

RASPUTIN:

And with just about everyone else in the court apparently. (THIS IS A DIRTY INNUENDO JOKE, SO PLAY FOR LAUGHS.)

ALL:

(SING AND DANCE) By the rivers of Babylon.
            Where we sat down.   *(Copyright Boney M 1976)*

COUNT TOTALANDUTTERNOBENDFARTYBREATHSKY:

Sire.

TSAR:

Yes Count Totalandutternobendfartybreathsky?

COUNT TOTALANDUTTERNOBENDFARTYBREATHSKY:

Oh nothing. It doesn't matter.

ENTER A SOLDIER.

SOLDIER:
Tsar, Tsar, we're losing the First World War.

TSAR:
The **First** World War you say—how do you know there's going to be another one?
THE THREE COUNTS STEP FORWARD.

THE THREE COUNTS:
Sire, we are your willing servants in this terrible war.

TSAR:
Good, find me a German to surrender to.

RASPUTIN (VERY ANGRY):
Look! will somebody *please* give me a blow job!

SOLDIER:
Tsar, the soldiers have formed soviets, they're planning revolution!

EVERYONE (TURNING TO AUDIENCE):
Watch out Mrs Thatcher, it could happen to *you.*

TSAR (SHOCKED):
Revolution? But I am the little holy fatherkin, and the people are my beloved
children.

SOLDIER:
But don't you see Tsar, you shouldn't have told them that all soldiers are
crapophiles and you bloody well hoped they all got killed and lost the war and
that you were going to make food illegal and legalise peasant hunting, because
you hated everyone who was common.

TSAR:
Bloody hell, can't they take a joke!

THE THREE COUNTS:
(SING AND DANCE) Brown girl in the ring tralala la la.
                 She like the sugar in the plum, plum plum.
                 (Copyright Boney M 1977)

TSAR (VERY UPSET, COLLAPSES ONTO KNEES):

I have lost Russia for my son.

COUNT BASTARDSKY:

By the way, how is the little bleeder? (THIS IS A BIG HISTORICAL JOKE SO PLAY FOR LAUGHS.)

RASPUTIN (WALKING ACROSS TO KNEELING TSAR):

Nicholas! An emperor must never kneel, but since you're down there, give us a blow job.
ENTER THE SPIRIT OF CLIFF RICHARD.

CLIFF RICHARD:

Decadence, decay, exploitation! Get down kids, it's 1917! I have not been born yet, but my spirit wills REVOLUTION!!!

LENIN AND TROTSKY RUSH ON AND START BOPPING EVERYONE, EVERYONE BOPS BACK, BY DAWN THEY HAVE BOPPED 'TIL THEY DROPPED AND LENIN AND TROTSKY ARE IN CONTROL. THE SPIRIT OF CLIFF REAPPEARS.

CLIFF RICHARD:

There you go guys, the world's first workers' state. Now don't bish it by letting Stalin have it.

LENIN AND TROTSKY:

No way Cliffy boy!
THE SPIRIT OF CLIFF DISAPPEARS.

LENIN:

This is brilliant, right Trotsky? The minute all those other countries stop invading us we can build a beautiful state, with trees and flowers and enough food and no war, and oh, everything! (HE SKIPS ABOUT A BIT.)

TROTSKY:

Great idea, Len, I'll go and get the first five year plan (HE IS ABOUT TO).

LENIN (CLUTCHING HEAD):

Oh no, I'm having a brain haemorrhage (TROTSKY RUNS OVER AND CRADLES LENIN IN HIS ARMS, INCIDENTALLY THIS IS A NOBLE AND BRAVE THING TO DO AND IN NO WAY GIRLY).

TROTSKY (WEEPING):

Len, Len, don't die, not now, we need you so much, you selfish bastard.

STALIN CREEPS ON FROM BEHIND WITH AN ICE AXE, THIS IS YOUR OPPORTUNITY FOR A BIT OF 'PANTO' KIDS, LENIN SHOULD GASP 'HE'S BEHIND YOU' AND TROTSKY SHOULD TURN AND SAY 'WHAT?' BUT STALIN HAS ALREADY RUN ROUND THE OTHER SIDE. SEE IF YOU CAN GET THE WHOLE AUDIENCE INVOLVED. LENIN WOULD HAVE APPROVED OF SUCH A DEMONSTRATION OF CO-OPERATION AND SOLIDARITY.

LENIN DIES.

TROTSKY:

Oh no! Lenin's life has reached its historically inevitable dialectical conclusion.

STALIN:

And so's yours (RAISES PICKAXE).

TROTSKY:

What are you doing, Stalin?

STALIN:

Everyone says you're so clever, I'm pickin' your brains (THIS IS A BRILL PUN SO PLAY IT FOR LAUGHS).

STALIN KILLS TROTSKY. THE THREE COUNTS REAPPEAR DRESSED AS WORKERS, MARCHING IN A FASCIST MANNER.

STALIN:

I am the Red Tsar!

TSAR: (GETTING UP)

Nothing has changed.

RASPUTIN:

In that case, give us a blow job, Joe.

THE THREE WORKERS:

(SING AND DANCE) Long time ago in Bethlehem
The Holy Bible say.   *(Copyright Boney M 1978)*

ENTER HITLER.

HITLER:

Hallo Stalin, how about a non-aggression pact?

STALIN:

Cheeky thing, Hitler. I hardly know you.

HITLER:

That's not what you said in the back of the bike-shed!

ALL:

What?!

HITLER:

Yes, it's true—I'm pregnant and you're the father, Stalin!

STALIN:

Blimey.

HITLER:

Oh no! I'm having a baby! (PRODUCES BABY FROM UNDER JACKET.) It's a girl—what shall we call it?

ALL:

Mrs Thatcher!!

RE-ENTER THE SPIRIT OF CLIFF RICHARD.

CLIFF:

And so Stalin and Hitler gave birth to Mrs Thatcher, and the historical dynasty of complete and utter nazis was assured. So remember, kids, revolution is a precious thing; don't let Mrs Thatcher stick her pickaxe in your trotskies. (THIS IS ANOTHER VAGUE INNUENDO GAG, SO GO FOR A LAUGH IF YOU CAN, BUT REMEMBER IT IS ALSO THE CONCLUSION TO THE WHOLE PLAY.)

THE WHOLE CAST LINK HANDS AND SING 'POWER TO ALL OUR FRIENDS'

(After this the director should get on stage and do a big speech of thanks to Rick for writing such a brilliant play.)

⊕ At the chemists

Mike the Cool Person is here to tell you that sniffing glue is bloody stupid. I mean it, bloody stupid. I tried it once, and quite apart from the fact that it made me want to throw up and eat my own belly button, I got my finger stuck when I picked my nose. Most embarrassing.

On the other hand, guys and gals (Vyvyan thinks my Jimmy Savile impression is fabulous) there are many totally safe drugs. Here is just a small selection of the many substances that I have sold to Neil, at enormous profit, under the catch-all title, DOPE:

> *Rabbit poo.*
>
> *Oxo cubes*
>
> *The brown square out of my water colour paint box*
>
> *The brown bits out of Rick's under-pants*
>
> *The Houses of Parliament*

It is a fact that to this day Neil considers the Houses of Parliament to be his 'stash' and the minute he can find a big enough fag paper, he's going to go to London and skin them up. Basically, there's nothing wrong with drugs, as long as you're selling them to Neil.

God damn the pusher man, signed Neil.

HOW TO CLEAN YOUR HOUSE

METHOD ONE
Make Neil do it.

METHOD TWO
Move.

METHOD THREE
Try not to think about it.

METHOD FOUR
Do it tomorrow.

**FIVE WORDS
PEOPLE
OFTEN THINK
ARE DIRTY:**

1 **Fishpaste**
2 **Masticate**
3 **Conservative**
4 **Dinty**
5 **Shit**

The history of POP

PART THREE

THE SIXTIES

That sun! That shimmering sixties sun, it seemed to shine on a decade and on a generation, lighting up the beautiful sounds of beautiful '67. It warmed and covered those far-away young people like an enormous star-spangled duvet. And it shone on Woodstock.

Woodstock was where the flower and love generation came of age, a quarter of a million gentle pilgrims drifted together in peace, took drugs and took their clothes off.

And dug the music, oh yes, they dug the music.

It happened! It really happened! Go ask your mum, she may have been there.

The Beatles had just finished their set, and John Lennon strolled to the front of the stage: 'Thank you,' he said, 'and thanks for the trousers, Auntie Nellie.'

Ecstasy!

John Lennon had said something dry, witty and unfathomable! The crowd could scarcely express the joy they felt. 'What were "the trousers"?' they thought. 'Who is Auntie Nellie? What had John meant?'

Almost as if by magic, the crowd knew; they understood John's cryptic message. Of course! It was all so clear: 'the trousers' were Woodstock itself, and 'Auntie Nellie' was . . . Cliff Richard, the man who had made it all possible, by inventing pop music. John Lennon, speaking with the voice of a whole generation, had paid tribute to the king, Cliff Richard.

In the very front row, John's Auntie Nellie smiled to herself, the new trousers she had knitted for him looked lovely in the lights.

Later that evening a Hell's Angel exploded in the crowd, covering twelve hippies in beer sick. The sixties were over.

And that's how it happened.

On the road

Rick writes:

That's right – we're talking about the Summer Hols – twelve weeks with nothing to do – 'cos any student who's at all cool doesn't bother with that sissy reading list or some poncy summer job that Daddy got him at his factory to get useful grass roots experience for later on when he'll have a career in Industrial management – ie, being a complete and utter bastard. No – there comes a time in every young adult's life when he just wants to hit the road (not literally) with only his rucksack on his back and his thumb in his hand or possibly with his student inter-rail ticket in his back pocket and his Youth Hostel Association membership card in his wallet along with his traveller's cheques, some local currency and his Mum's Visa Card, but aside from that, and possibly his car or maybe an airline ticket to Greece and one of those great pink and black sausage bags from Flip that fold up really small when they're empty but are really great for putting all the dead Italian shoes you're bound to buy with your Mum's Visa Card in.

There are two places you can go on holiday.

1 Great Britain
2 Abroad

Abroad has the advantages of

a) *more cred,* eg. 'Hey, what did you do last summer?' 'Oh, I hitched down to Athens with a Swedish chick, went to a couple of pretty heavy demos, got arrested, beaten up by the pigs, saw the Acropolis in Son et Lumière and got deported.'

b) *Better weather*, a disadvantage if you've got horrible pale skin like people with red hair have.

c) *Cheaper* – unless you hitch down to Athens with a Swedish chick who turns out to be a forty-year-old transvestite and nicks all your cash and then you go on a demo and some bastard, pretending to be one of the kids but he's really a pickpocket, swipes your traveller's cheques and then you get arrested by the pigs and you have to wait three hours to phone your parents and get them to wire you some money and then you have to give most of it to the pigs and also pay for your airfare just because the Establishment decided to deport you 'cos you're too anarchic for them to handle and then you get back and your father makes you take a job in his factory to pay him back for the money you borrowed and because he says it'll be good grass roots experience for later when you leave college and take up a career in industrial management.

Holidays in Great Britain have the following advantages

a) Television, you won't be lying on a sunny beach wondering whether John Craven's had another hair transplant

b) More cred, eg 'Hey what did you do last summer?' 'Oh, I took the tube down to Brixton and hung out on the front-line and nearly got hassled by the pigs'

c) It's easier to phone home

EUROPE ON 10p A DAY

Can't be done.

HITCHIN'

NEIL, MR HITCH, THE KING OF THE ROAD, SPEAKS OUT

Power. There's nothing quite like hitching. Standing beside roads is similar to bits of it, and riding along in cars is similar to other bits, but only hitching itself sums up the total experience.

All you need for successful hitching, is a thumb, some clothes (nobody picks up a nudie hippy) AND LOTS OF TIME! It's no good standing beside a road with your thumb out thinking, 'Oh no way man! Bummer! If I don't get a lift to the stock exchange soon, like my multi-national company Amalgamated Breadheads will collapse!' If that's where your head is at, buy a car.

PEOPLE WHO SHOULDN'T HITCH

People carrying vital transplant organs from one hospital to another.
People who say things like 'time is money' and 'you're fired Jones'.
People with no thumbs.

PEOPLE WHO SHOULD HITCH

Heads.
Freaks.
People who say things like, 'Oh, look at that amazing blade of grass. I hope no cars come for hours, so I can watch it grow.'

THINGS TO THINK WHILE YOU'RE WAITING

'Hope I get a lift soon'.

'Hope it doesn't rain/stops raining'.

'Wow, imagine if I got picked up by some amazing freak chick, in a VW caravanette with purple crush velvet cushions, and eight foot long spliffs and a video.'

'Remember that amazing lift when that guy picked me up right outside college and it turned out he was actually going past my bedroom! Incredible, two hundred miles and he actually dropped me off on the landing upstairs at my old lady's! And he had 'Dark Side of the Moon' on tape.

HITCHING STORIES

This last thought brings me onto an essential part of hitching, the re-telling of hitching stories, with your freak mates.

Here is an example.

'Oh it was amazing, got this amazing lift in a mini up the A34 to the M4 and did the whole M4 in three lifts, had a bit of a wait at junction 14 but after Bristol it was amazingly quick getting on the M5 going north – this lorry took me all the way to Birmingham and dropped me at those services, you know. It was incredible, I just stuck out my thumb, this Golf pulls up. I says M6, Manchester. He says, "Jump in." He dropped me on the Knutsford services, so I needed a lift to get me onto the A356 ...'

This is a good example of part of a hitching story, at the end of it (in about two hours) all the other freaks will say, 'Sounds amazing' and everyone will have another half of cider and blackcurrant.

PEOPLE WHO GIVE YOU LIFTS

Almost by definition people who give lifts, have cars, which means only one thing, ACCESS TO BREAD. Hitching is a two-way thing, every freak needs a straight to pick him up, the lion lies down with the lamb.

● *SALES PEOPLE:* The most common lift of all is from the company rep who will be driving a company Sierra, with his company jacket on a hanger, and his company mouth will spew. totally uncool fascist vibes at you, like 'I normally give lifts because it can get boring driving as much as I do.' Don't be fooled, he is trying to CHANGE YOUR HEAD. Company reps are not reps at all, but government agents, scouring the country trying to turn all the freaks into straights. *Do not accept sweets from these people, they are almost certainly spiked with white sugar.*

● *EX-HEADS:* This is also a very common type of lift. It will be in a Dianne or a VW Beetle, and the groover will lay some totally depressing vibe on you like, 'I always give lifts because I hitched myself when I was a student.' That is your cue to lay a big *conversion* trip on them, like, 'So what turned you into a straight man, you're talking like a freak, but really you've got a breadhead car, breadhead jeans and a breadhead enormous AA book of the road. You're a *vibe traitor* man! Worse than a pig!' This sort of thing can shorten your life considerably, but you have to do it – being a freak is not a fair weather thing, it doesn't stop when you leave college.

● *A TRANSIT FULL OF GREASERS:* Do not, under any circumstances, accept a lift from a Transit full of greasers. Even if you've been stuck in the same place for fifteen years. A little guy with long hair and glasses will be driving, you could almost take him for a freak. 'Hop in the back man,' he'll say, and too late you will find yourself staring at twelve thirty-five-year-old dead heads all working on bits of a Harley Davidson with sick in their beards, and chains on their denim jerkins that they wear over their piss-soaked leather jackets. 'Hallo man,' one will say, 'Got any dope?' and then they'll nick your stash, and pass you a bottle of Woodpecker, and you have to take a swig, even though they've all got scabs like cornflakes all over their mouths, so you do, and it turns out that the Woodpecker bottle is their TOILET, and you've just drunk a mouthful of greaser piss! 'Great man, now you're one of us,' says one with a dead chicken stapled to his jeans, then he gets out an axe and says, 'We share all our money,' so you give them all your bread. Then the one with the belly like he was pregnant and the sort of weeping, running sore on his chin that makes his beard drip, says 'I'm a right bleedin' bastard,' and you say, sort of lamely, 'Er great, I'm Neil,' and he says, 'D'you know what lads? I'm so horny I could almost de-bag the hippy,' and the other one says, 'Wacko, Gerald, let's all put our underpants on our heads!' and you suddenly realise – nightmare! – they're from Eton. And then you get really worried.

● *ANOTHER FREAK:* Karma-wise this is the most beautiful lift of all, you will share stashes and discuss vibes. Travel-wise it is a total bummer as the car will break down within five seconds of you getting in.

● ● ●

HIDING YOUR STASH WHEN HASSLED BY THE PIGS ON A MOTORWAY SLIP ROAD

Like all hyperstraights, pigs are really finnickity about cleanliness, their stomachs are easily turned, they will often ask a rank and steaming hippy to turn out his pockets, but *never* his bottom. Remember, 'a stash up the bum is worth two sewn into the turn-up'.

THINGS TO DO ON CAR JOURNEYS

1 Look out of the window
2 Feel sick
3 Do the crossword
4 Be sick
5 Clean up the car
6 Whine

LEAVES FROM THE SCRAP BOOK

LONE STUDENT SITS IN.

The refectory at Scumbag college was occupied this morning by Neil Pye, a lone student demonstrator. Mr Pye made a great commotion claiming that the college authorities were 'fascists' and 'bad vibe merchants'. He pledged that his protest would continue until something was done. Unfortunately, when Mr Pye was asked to explain his protest it suddenly became clear that he had completely forgotten. He slunk away pledging to be back when he remembered what had been worrying him.

A CURIOUS incident occurred on the public highway last night, when the police investigated a Yellow Ford Anglia which was apparently out of control. After a chase, the car came to rest in a lily pond, where the driver was discovered to be a hamster. In the passenger seat was Vyvyan Basterd, the hamster's owner. Although Mr Basterd and the hamster were both almost senselessly drunk, Mr Basterd was clearly the more inebriated of the two – this, he claimed was why he had asked the hamster to drive. Mr Basterd has been unable to comment since, as he is being sick almost continuously. The hamster was found to contain almost three times more vodka than the hamster limit and this morning magistrates banned it from driving for a year.

POETRY 82 reviewed by Rick.

made a lovely widow Twanky and Ralph Jobby did well as 'Jim'. Also Amanda Nice, Susy Good-bottom, Walter Snot and Rick made super fairies.

There were seven young poets giving readings at last night's concert and basically, six of them were complete crap. However one young genius was BRILLIANT, he single-handedly revitalised the British poetry scene. He read poetry of such beauty and significance that the whole audience had to leave almost immediately to get some fresh air. It is a tribute to the power of his work that none had the courage to return. His name? Genius needs no name. But it rhymes with Dick.

ASTOUNDING CLAIM!!! STUDENT SAYS HE IS THE TRUE FATHER OF PRINCE WILLIAM

ATTRACTIVE STUDENT, Mike TheCoolPerson made an astonishing claim yesterday when he alleged that he and the Princess of Wales, then, plain Diana Spencer had had a real "red hot bitch of a scene" going when he had been a post-graduate student in bed-wetting at the Young England kindergarten where the princess had worked, prior to the royal engagement.

Prince William

MIKE

'I AM PAUL McCARTNEY'S SON' CLAIMS PRETTY STUDENT MIKE

Pop star Paul McCartney was again plunged into a paternity row last night when student Mike claimed that he

helpful hints

N E I L ' S   A D D R E S S   S O C K .

Power. Have you ever lost an address book? Wow, is that a total freak out! I'd rather lose my virginity than lose my address book. Like, about a year ago, I lost my address book and like … MEGA PANIC!!! Thank God I hadn't written any addresses in it. But if I had, I would have like lost them too. But, well, you know, it seems a bit stupid to like not fill in your address book, just in case you lose it, so I have come up with a household hint on the subject. Write your addresses on something *you never take off.*

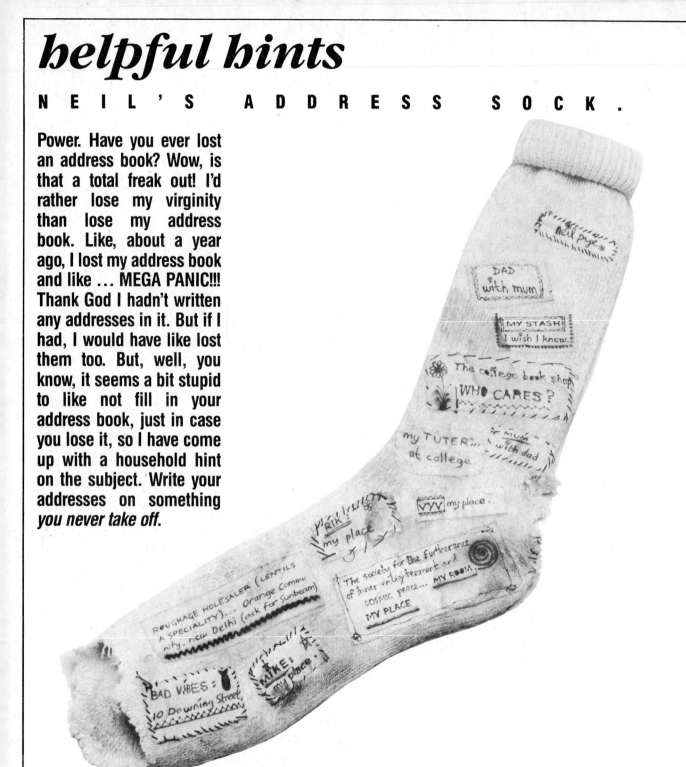

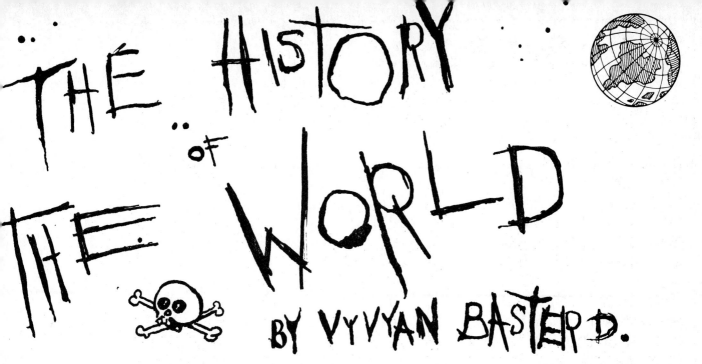

THE HISTORY OF THE WORLD

BY VYVYAN BASTERD.

GOOD EVENING YOU BASTARDS

Right. At the very beginning of absolutely everything ever, there was the most massive conceivable explosion. Absofuckinglootly huge it was and completely brilliant. If you can imagine drinking ten pints of paraffin, holding your breath for two hours, going out and eating a special vindaloo set meal for twelve (extra hot), jumping up and down vigorously for fifteen minutes, drinking a party seven of Nasties extra mild, setting the toilet on fire and rushing in to do a biggy, then that would be nothing compared to this banger.

Now sceptics will probably say, 'OK then, Jobbie-features, how come life was formed from a massive explosion, eh? Bit of a first for the Universe, isn't it? I thought that explosions tended on the whole to destroy things completely and utterly. Or perhaps I'm being very stupid and dull, I mean I have only got a degree in ballistics and got – Ow get off, that's my head.'

Yes, vilence is one solution, but the answer to their main question is simple and they obviously haven't spotted it because they're all total nerdies.

THE THEORY OF RELATIVITY

Einstein invented this, and he also invented the Atom Bomb so he must have been a pretty good bloke. The theory is as follows: TO EVERY ACTION THERE IS AN EQUAL AND OPPOSITE REACTION.

In other words, what Einstein invented was that every time an apple fell on his head somewhere else in the Universe there was another completely different apple which wasn't falling on his head.

AND THIS WAS COMPLETELY VITAL STUFF! It meant that, whenever anything was happening, the completely opposite was happening as well. (Like I'm writing this at the moment and you're not, for example, eg Motorhead wrote the Ace of Spades and the Nolan Sisters didn't at *exactly* the same time.) So when the Big Bang destroyed everything millions and billions of years ago, it also DIDN'T! Brilliant, eh? *(see fig. 1).*

Fig 1 *The Universe being completely destroyed and not being completely destroyed by the biggest explosion ever.*

THE ROMANS

The first thing that happened after the Big Bang was the Romans. They were a completely pathetic bunch of utter wankers who used to sit around eating grapes in the bath and inventing central heating. The only good thing they ever did was to invent gladiators and chariot racing. But because they were all so weedy, the Romans had to get other people to do all their fighting, racing, drinking, etc, and so they hauled in all these completely brilliant maniacs from the rest of Europe. Gauls, Visigoths, Vandals, Huns, Picts, Normans and, of course, the great Atilla the Hun, etc, and this was the greatest gang in the history of the world ever, and of course, once they got to Rome they saw how utterly wet and girly it was and smashed the whole place up completely. And that's pretty well the history of Rome. Good riddance to it, I say. Anyhow, the greatest achievement of the Roman period was to get out of the way in time for the most fantastic and hard period so far, ie, the **DARK AGES** (see fig. 2).

Fig 2 *The dark ages*

THE VIKING EMPIRE

It was the Vikings, in fact, the hardest and most brilliant of all the people who lived in this time, who wrote the first heavy metal song ever, 'Raping, Pillaging and Drinking Lager'. The Vikings drank a lot of lager and one night when they were completely pissed they invented the days of the week as a joke. Monday was named after a particularly violent and drink-crazed Viking chief called Mon who had two great horns growing out of his head. Mon used to do a lot of raping and pillaging in his spare time and it is from this that the word 'horny' originated. The rest of the days were split between his mates who were called Tues,

Wednes, Thurs, Fri and Satur, except for Sunday which was originally called Lagerday. This was later changed by a load of stupid bloody Christians who had invented a thing called Sunday school and wanted to give it lots of free publicity. Anyway, soon afterwards all the Vikings pissed off back to Denmark where by this time there was lots of great films about nuns and schoolgirls without much on.

The world was now a pretty boring place apart from a few wars, and even some of these were about stupid girly things like roses *(see fig. 3).*

Fig 3 *Even the wars were girly after the vikings left*

THE INDUSTRIAL REVOLUTION

And then suddenly, completely by surprise, like one of those real wiffers that accidentally escape at mealtimes, the IN-DUSTRIAL REVOLUTION happened. Now when history teachers tell you this was a really boring period, they are LYING. It was amazing and important and anyone who tells you it wasn't is asking for a toaster in the mouth, because it was during this time that all the mod cons that go to make present day life so comfortable were invented. Things like the Ford Anglia, the bayonet, surgery, electric guitars (big surge forward in Heavy Metal around this time), hard drugs, the destruction of boring great cissy tracts of natural landscape–oh yeah, while we're at this juncture, I might mention that this phase in history is not popular with hippies, freaks and all the Save The Stickleback girly type zeroes who always lie down in the path of PROGRESS (ie, the humane gassing of millions of woodland creatures to make way for a brilliant and highly dangerous Nuclear Reactor Factory, etc.) If you have trouble with these types while talking history, dear reader, then don't worry. I have the perfect answer to any of their arguments. It's called **the VYVYAN BASTERD QUITE UNNECESSARILY PAINFUL DEATH MACHINE** (see fig. 4).

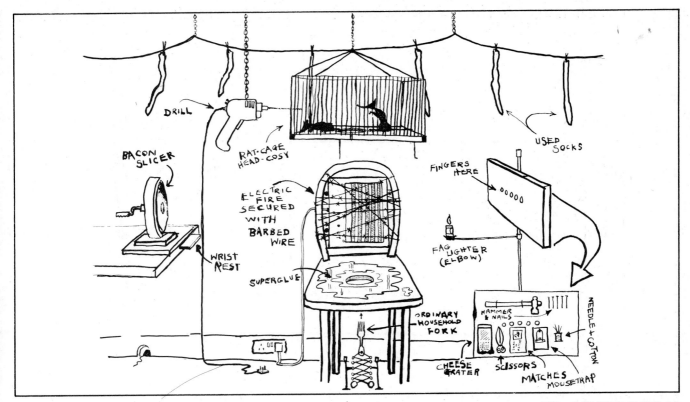

Fig 4 *T.V.B.Q.U.P.D.M.*

THE MODERN AGE

So the Industrial Revolution gave us all the great things that go to make up the last period of history, *THE MODERN AGE.* (This has got nothing to do with Mods who are wankers). And the three great things about the MODERN AGE ARE:

1 *Cars.* Especially yellow Ford Anglias with flames up the side.

2 *Telly.* Without which life would not be worth living.

3 *Everything else.* And cars again.

So if you like getting really drunk and watching video nasties while driving at 100 mph down the motorway, listening to the radio and a Sony headset and making a telephone call at the same time while undergoing neurosurgery from a robot, then this is the era for you.

An open poem to Felicity Kendall

FROM AN ADMIRER *(called Rick)*

Oh Felicity, Felicity,
You fill me with electricity.
But that does not mean that you are shocking.
Oh no, you are nice,
Like sugar and spice,
Like a proper girly ought to be.
   (Even though I am sure you have radical views
   on the subject of equal opportunities.)
Your second name is Kendall.
Which if you jumble up all the letters,
And take some away,
And add some others,
Makes 'I love you'.
I adored you as the star of TV's 'The Good Life'
And I'm not being sexist, but you'd make a 'good wife'
How about it Filly?

This is a brilliant poem. But brilliant poems do not grow on trees (unless of course they're written on apples), so I have decided to show you all how to write brilliant poetry.

First of all, here are some reproductions of the *actual pages* from my rough book in which the early drafts of 'Felicity Kendall' were developed. Here you see the tortured mind at work. Of course, none of you will ever be as good a poet as me, because I'm brilliant, and you're a bunch of nob ends, but anyway.

Oh Felicity, Felicity,

Your name rhymes with ~~electricity~~.....

Felicity
Electricity
Synchronicity?
Police?
PIG?
Bacon?

"You are like bacon
Because I want to
eat you at breakfast"

~~Oh Felicity Felicity,~~

~~You fill me with~~ ← Shocking? better word

~~electricity.~~

~~Like putting your nob in a plug socket.~~

~~Except you~~

~~Haven't got one.~~

~~A nob that is, I'm sure you have a plug socket,~~

~~Or how would you play your brilliant 'Shape up and Dance'~~

~~Aerobics record?~~

~~You wouldn't, that's how......~~

TOO LONG

DOSNT RHYME

Oh Felicity, Felicity,

You fill me with

Electricity.

Isn't that shocking? GOOD ✓✓✓✓✓

Your timeless silken loveliness is so smashing,

I want to wander through it, gorgeously naked,

unashamed of the spots on my bottom.

← Save for novel

You are so nice

Without crabs or lice,

Like a proper girly ought to be.

Watch out! remember what Trotsky said about sexists!

✓✓✓
Good Life
Good Wife
BRILLIANT
✓✓✓✓

Your second name is Kendall.

~~You are like the mint cake.~~

~~Cool, fresh, and nice to suck.~~

If I had a tin of

Alphabetti Spaghetti,

Have got a tin of
Alphabeti Sphagetti, under
bed, locked in suitcase - remember
TRUTH IN POETRY!

I'd spell 'I love you' GOOD phrase, keep in

Before I ate it.

How about a quick bonk?

TOO RAUNCHY

Some useful rhymes to use in writing Poems

- words that rhyme with 'dog':
  - **DOG**
  - **NOB** (para rhyme)
  - **SOCIALISM** (only to be used in modern verse)

- words that rhyme with 'pig':   words that rhyme with 'pavement':
  - **PIG**   **PAVEMENT**
                                                                      TROTSKY

THE WORD 'TROTSKY' IN POETRY

The word 'Trotsky' in poetry is like a 'wild card' in poker. It can be used almost anywhere, but should be employed sparingly, and with care. There are many examples in poetry where the word Trotsky would have improved the work.

'My love is like a red red Trotsky'

'I wandered lonely as a Trotsky'

'Dulce et Decorum Est Pro Patria Trotsky'

*'Half a league, half a league, half a league Trotsky'**

* Half-a-League Trotsky is believed to be a reference to the famous Bolshevik's younger brother Vlad who was enormously well blessed in the trouser department.

● **words that rhyme with 'trotsky'**

BROTSKY   DROTSKY
CROTSKY   FROTSKY.

YOU NOW HAVE ENOUGH INFORMATION TO BEGIN WRITING POETRY
YOURSELF. HERE IS AN EXAMPLE OF A PIECE OF RHYMING VERSE:

Today, I saw a dog,
Yes, a dog.
Talking to a pig,
Yes, a pig.
They were on the pavement,
Discussing Trotsky.
Not brotsky or crotsky or drotsky or frotsky.
But Trotsky.

F O L K L O R E

Olde rhyme reason and learning that is still true today.

'If enough lager you do sup
 rest assured you will throw up' Monk D'Wally D'Honk. 1485 (cans a night)

'Hot water and a sponge, with a bit of bleach on it,
 Is quite a good way to clean up vomit' Mrs D'Wally D'Honk (small port and lemon)

'If you've got a screaming big headache, a mouthful of carpet and you're surrounded by
 empty beers cans, then it's morning' Vyvyan 1984.

Five club acts people often think are dirty:

1 Big Mike Pugh and his Talking Big-Jobs
2 Gavin Hatemail and the 'Don't Tell The Wife' Dancers
3 Ralph 'Spot the ball' Harrison
4 'Uncle' Nobby Lewis and his unusual impressions (Featuring TV's famous
  'God help us, who dropped that one?' quiz)
5 'Stretchy' Marc Morrison and Paul

and how to use one.

Sooner or later you will have to go to the launderette – like treading in dog do, it happens to us all. When you do go, you will soon discover that there are two kinds of launderette, terrible, and bloody terrible. Either way, you lose.

● **MOVE ONE** get all your dirty stuff together. This is essential, if you neglect this simple first rule, all your subsequent weary efforts will go to waste. Remember: GOING TO THE LAUNDERETTE IS NOT ENOUGH, YOU *MUST* TAKE YOUR DIRTY CLOTHES WITH YOU.

Launderette rule A: states that whenever you go to the launderette, you will always forget to take exactly half the things that need washing. Unfortunately...

Launderette rule B: states that you will always return with only half the things you took. So at the end of the day, you will be left with only a quarter of your entire clothes stash clean, and ready to wear. Work it out, it's a bitch.

● **MOVE TWO** okay, the filth is in the sack, (and that doesn't mean a policeman with a bag on his head). For God's sake get out of the house quick!! This is the point at which so many dreams and schemes evaporate. It's so easy to sit down and think, 'Well I've got it all into a sack, that's a pretty positive and together thing to have done. I can relax for a bit.' NEVER REST ON YOUR LAURELS! Six months later you will be fishing around in the same steaming sack,

searching for a sock that you've only worn twelve times.

● **MOVE THREE** Launderettes are essentially boring places. How do you spot one?

What to look for

Washing machines
Tumble driers

What to avoid

Freezers full of food, racks of newspapers and magazines, shiny new cars behind plate glass windows
Mounds of fruit with men in cloth caps shouting 'Apples ten pence a pound'

IF YOU HAVE A WEAK HEART, BEWARE! As you walk down the street towards the hell hole, you will be muttering 'I hope there's a machine free' over and over again, your heart will beat faster and your pulse will quicken. You will go in and LO! there will be six million empty machines! and every single one will say OUT OF ORDER on a scrappy bit of paper, crammed into the coin slot, and your heart will stop, and you will eat your own trousers in frustration.

Yeah! OK, join the queue for a machine. And while you're waiting, read the cards on the boards: 'For sale, a lawn mower'. DIG IT!! that is kinky sex! Anyone who is street and cool knows that all cards on notice boards are for real good sex stuff.

● **You just gotta know the code.**

> Furniture restored by local craftsman. Re-upholstering etc.

A **In street-wise gay talk, a guy's 'furniture' means the backs of his knees, and 'restoration' means the smearing on and licking off of peanut butter. 'Re-upholstering means the guy recently bought some new Y fronts, and 'etc' means he keeps on licking till his tongue gets tired.**

> LOST TIBBLES, MUCH LOVED TABBY CAT, £5 REWARD FOR INFORMATION

B **'Much loved' means just what it says, some pimp's lost the number one feline attraction from his sex menagerie, and wants it back and is prepared to pay.**

> Third female wanted to share house. Own room, share all bills.

C **This translates directly as 'Madame Blam has an enormous fridge and for extra naughty little boys, she'll get the daffodils out. Also all invoices that arrive are to be split up equally'.**

Right, so finally there's a machine free. Grab the filthy sack with the horrid stuff in it, (and I don't mean Rick's scrotum!) and load up the machine!

Launderette rule C: There are more loose pubes in one launderette than there are atoms in the universe.
An interesting story is connected with this rule.

The interesting story of Papyrus the slave.

Long long ago, in ancient Babylon the king was most distressed because try as the royal washers might, they could not achieve that 'blue white, lemon, april freshness' that the king desired whenever he got chocolate, blood and understains on his raiment. Then one day, Papyrus the slave invented New Formula Skidoo and it was brill.
So the King said to Papyrus, 'How can I repay you? Gold, Jewels?' And Papyrus, who was a clever bastard said, 'All I want Majesty, is one pair of Y fronts, for every pube to be found in the royal launderette.' The king thought, 'That's easy – bet there aren't more than twelve.' But there were four in the first soap compartment, and eight stuck to the fluffy old sock behind the end drier and a couple in one of the coin slots, and some in the lost clothes basket, and in the end over six billion pubes were discovered in that one small royal launderette.

The king was bankrupted, and Papyrus, who now owned every pair of Y fronts in Babylon, changed his name to Marks and Spencer.
And that's how it happened.

● MOVE FIVE
Going for change. Launderette rule D:

States that there will be no change in the shop and you will not have brought any. This means that you will have to go out to buy some small item in order to get some change. It is at this point that you discover that the launderette is on an enormous industrial estate, and the only shop is a furniture warehouse. You will then have to buy a £300 sofa in order to obtain two 50p bits.

NOW THE WASH IS OVER, AND IT'S OVER FOR YOU TOO. NO DRYING SCENE, NO CLEAN CLOTHES SCENE, NO HAPPY ENDING SCENE, AND WHY? BECAUSE YOU DIDN'T READ THE LABEL ON THAT INNOCENT LOOKING HANKY, DID YOU?

What? you don't know what ⚠70° means? Well ⚠70° means 'Do not machine wash this item as it totally fucks up everything else, and dyes them the wrong colour'

And you left a quid in the back pocket of your jeans.

'I RECKON THAT IF I COLLECTED UP ALL THE BOGIES THAT HAD EVER COME OUT OF MY NOSE, I'D NEVER GET THEM ALL BACK UP THERE. SO LIKE, I'M NOT EVEN GOING TO TRY IT.' neil '77

-QUICK CROSSWORDS

1

DOWN

1 Ruthless, unfeeling dictator/mends roof with dried grass (8)

ACROSS

1 Legalise It! (4)
2 Small, smelly, one of the four million (4,3)

2

DOWN

1 Polite term for horrid smelly noisy thing that comes out of your trousers (6,4)
2 Horrid smelly silent thing that comes out of your trousers (6,6)

ACROSS

1 Common term for horrid smelly noisy thing that comes out of trousers (4)
2 Has same effect on you as horrid smelly noisy thing that comes out of your trousers (3,8)
3 Another term for horrid smelly noisy thing that comes out of your trousers (4)

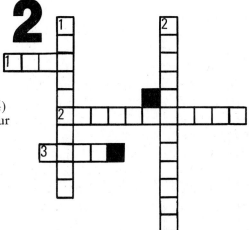

3

DOWN

1 Where Rick goes to 'read' the underwear ads in Cosmopolitan (3,6)

ACROSS

1 Who crawled out of the toilet to lead the Conservative party? (8)

1
Down – ① Yor
ACROSS – ① think ② those are

2
Down – ① The ② answer
ACROSS – ① Well ② they're ③ not

3
DOWN – ① Save breath so ① work it out yourself Thatcher!
ACROS –

FUN WITH FIREARMS

Good morning. You know what they say, if you've got a gun, you're going to have fun. And here's one of my all time favourites— **THE NOISY PISS ROUTINE**

1. Take a concealed handgun to a busy local public lavvy.

2. Bet someone £10 that you can piss a lot louder than they can.

3. Sneak the barrel of your revolver out of your zip and LET THE LAVVY HAVE IT!

4. And there's your vodka money . . . easy as pissing against a wall and ten times as dangerous.

PASS THE TIME,

A COMPENDIUM OF JOLLY WAYS TO PLAY WITH YOURSELF

THE 'TRUTH' GAME
Send Neil out of the room and then everybody decide to be Neil, call Neil back in and say 'guess who we are, Neil, we're a boring, useless little shit called Neil', see how long it takes him to guess who you are.
(NB Every household has a 'Neil')

MURDER IN THE DARK
Turn off all the lights and kill someone.

SARDINES
Good way to get a free snog.

SNOGGING
Not a particularly good way to get a free sardine.

WHY AUSTRALIA IS CRAP:

1 ● The Sex Pistols didn't come from there.
2 ● It's too far away.
3 ● I don't like it.

'**NEVER** CHANT YOUR MANTRA WHILE EATING LENTIL STEW, IT GETS YOUR T-SHIRT DIRTY.'

neil '81

BEING POPULAR

Hello people, it's me.

A great way to impress your friends is by answering back to leading figures in the pop scene when you are listening to them on the radio. Remember to shout quite loudly and wave your arms about because your friends might be really into the music and therefore difficult to distract. But the effect is great. It shows that—

a You are on really intimate terms with lots of rock stars (NB. avoid abusing Marilyn for this reason ho, hum.)

b You are really quick-witted and ought to be on TV or something. But anyway, enough about me—here are some of the extraordinary things I've said to Rock Stars on the radio...

Rod Stewart: **'Do ya think I'm sexy?'**
Me: **'No, I bloody well don't, big nose!'**

Boy George: **'Do you really want to hurt me?'**
Me: **'Yes!'**

Mick Jagger: **'I can't get no satisfaction.'**
Me: **'I'm not surprised big lips, you're so old and out of touch with the kids that even a can of Cydrax would probably give you a runny bottom. And nineteen heart attacks. Har har, did you hear what I said everybody?'** *(Repeat if necessary)*

Another graet way to increase your popularity (especially with the wilder side of today's youth and blimey I know some real hell raisers I can tell you! My friend Tim deliberately burned a cigarette hole in one of my library books last week–IN A LECTURE!!! He's just totally potty! They should make a film about some of the things we all get up to they really should!) Anyway, another way is of course that great rebel-rocker tradition–the PRACTICAL JOKE. Here's some of the ones I and my dotty pals (we call ourselves 'The Silly Billies From Hell') have got up to in the past–and some of the ones that were too wild even for us lot!

● 1 THE LAUNDERETTE SHOCKER

One of your friends goes into a launderette and sits there pretending to do his washing. Meanwhile, you go to a greengrocers and buy a small punnet of raspberries. Put one of the raspberries down your trousers and scoff the rest. Then rush into the launderette shouting, 'Look out everyone, I've got raspberries in my pants!' Whereupon your chum leaps up and says, 'Prove it, nerdy' and you whip the raspberry out to everyone's amazement, shouting, 'It's a blummen good thing I'm in a launderette then, isn't it everybody!!!'. Then run away.

● 2 BATMAN

Go up to a total stranger in the street and say 'Hello, I'm Batman'. When they look totally bewildered and outwitted, pretend you've got it wrong and shout 'Oh no, I've got it wrong, I meant to say "Hello, you're a FAT MAN!!!"'. Then laugh at them and run away.
I've tried this one several times, and

sometimes I take along a little cassette recorder so that I and the rest of the Silly Billies can have a good old chortle when we get back to my pad afterwards. Here are a couple of hilarious transcripts for you to enjoy too.

► ► ►

◆◆◆

'Batman tapes. High Street. 11.45am Sat. 19th May 1984.'

(SOUND OF RUNNING FEET AND PANTING)

RICK: It's on, it's on. Get off it Geoffrey.

GEOFFREY: It's not, spazzy!

RICK: It bloody is! Look the thing's going round.

TIM: Quick, there's an old square coming out of Debenhams.

RICK: I should have bet you a hundred pounds or something like that then Geoffrey — you were utterly wrong then weren't you?

GEOFFREY: That's for me to know and you to worry about isn't it, farty.

TIM: Oh, put a nob in it for flip's sake you types — get that old square and freak him out before he escapes into Sainsburys.

GEOFFREY: Yes, go on Rick, it's your turn —

RICK: It is not! I did the last one.

GEOFFREY: You ruddy didn't! You pretended to fall over just before you got up to that old lady and said you couldn't do it because your leg was nearly bleeding.

TIM: Come on, come on — he's getting away.

RICK: Wait a minute — I've got a better idea. Why don't we take it in turns to go and stand in the middle of the plaza next to the lottery and shout 'I've just done a really smelly fart. Sorry everybody'? Brilliant! You go first Geoffrey.

TIM: No. Go and Batman that pensioner turdy, or I'll tell the rest of the guys in the pub tonight how you asked that girl in the chemist for a thousand packets of Jimmies because you didn't know the proper dirty word for Durex.

RICK: Oh no! The tape-recorder's suddenly broken!

(SOUND OF TAPE-RECORDER BEING SWITCHED OFF)

◆◆◆

'Batman Tapes. High Street. 12.00am Sat. 19th May 1984.'

RICK: Right, it's running now, Neil — go.

NEIL: Eh?

RICK: Go!

NEIL: Oh. OK. See you.

RICK: Come back!

NEIL: Eh?

RICK: Where are you going?

NEIL: I don't know. It was you who told me to go—

RICK: I mean start.

NEIL: Eh?

RICK: Oh God, I thought I explained all this. You just pretend to be a normal member of the public, right, and I tell you I'm Batman.

NEIL: I am a normal member of the public.

RICK: SO WHAT'S THE PROBLEM???

NEIL: All right all right, don't get heavy. I'll just pretend to be me.

RICK: NO!! I've told you—you've got to pretend to be someone else. It's got to sound like I've gone up to a complete stranger in the street.

NEIL: So why don't you just like go up to a complete stranger in the street?

RICK: I've told you. Because I'm not feeling very well.

NEIL: You're scared aren't you?

RICK: I'm not bloody scared!

(SOUND OF A HEAVY BLOW)

NEIL: Oooooww! Wow Rick, that hurt.

RICK: Now who's scared, farty features?

NEIL: Oh wow, I can't see properly.

RICK: Look, can we get on with this please?

NEIL: I don't know. I'm feeling really bad now.

RICK: JUST SHUT UP! We're running out of bloody tape now so for flip's sake let's get started. I say hello to you first, right?

NEIL: OK.

RICK: Right…Hello.

NEIL: Right. And now I pretend to be someone else.

RICK: We've started, Neil.

NEIL: I know, I'm just getting my bit together.

RICK: OH GOD!! Look.. I'll start again. Hello.

NEIL: Er…like…Bonjour Monsieur Rick, what's happening?

RICK: I'm Batman.

NEIL: Wow. Le amazing. Bonjour Monsieur Bathomme. Comment allez-vous like, at the moment?

RICK: Oh no! I've got it wrong! I meant to say 'Hello, you're a FAT MAN!!' ''

NEIL: Oh shit. Do we have to start again then? Ow! Ow! Ow!

CLICK

'WHY I WANT TO MARRY PRINCE ANDREW'

by VYVYAN

He's got a helicopter.
He would offer me no intellectual threat.
I'd like to be a top model and association with him would boost my career.

NUDIE VYV PICS EXCLUSIVE!!!!

Wow! is the Queen going to be pissed off! Here are the first ever nudie bum shots of Prince Andrew's attractive model boyfriend Vyvyan. The pictures are definitely genuine and were sold to us by a man who called himself 'Rick, no, Neil'.

'I HAVE ONLY MET Prince Andrew once and I told him he was a blood sucking parasite,' said lovely model boy Vyv as he left his home yesterday. 'If we made love, I certainly don't remember.'

JUST WHAT THE DOCTOR ORDERED!!!

GORGEOUS VYV used to be a medical student, but since he changed to modelling, things have really been 'getting better'. He's a real tonic, isn't he girls? Bet he's making your temperature rise. Recently lovely Vyv's name has been linked with Prince Andrew's. Let's hope Vyv gets him on the slab and gives him an anal enema real soon!

'I am not jealous of Vyvyan,' said jilted Koo Stark yesterday.

'Of course we've known for ages,' grinned flat-mate Rick, but we promised not to tell, I'll never forget, I was weeing on Neil's bed when Vyv rushed in and told

The history of POP

PART FOUR

'KICK THIS BUM OUT OF THE COUNTRY'

'We have informed Mr Richard's manager that permission for the use of our Town Hall has been withdrawn. His is not the sort of act we want in our town'
The Mayor of Guildford.

In the early summer of 1977, Cliff Richard embarked on his notorious Anarchy in the Home Counties tour. The Peter Pan of pop had claws! Cliff had been worrying about all the things young kids worry about – unemployment, the pigs, high rise, spray on boredom! Even his Saturday evening TV show with Una Stubbs, seemed to say one thing: *NO FUTURE!* 'I'm bored,' he remarked to Hank Marvin one day as he and the Shadows dropped a pound and a half of talcum powder, 'I'm going to call myself "Cliffy Bastard!" and sing a song called "Balls bum poo piss".'

Punk Rock had been invented.

What an extraordinary summer. Cliff's first single ever to be banned by the BBC. Sue Barker banned from Wimbledon for wearing a dustbin liner. Una Stubbs banned from 'Give Us a Clue' for miming 'Deep Throat'. Tommy Steele was arrested in Los Angeles for gobbing on the Jimmy Carson show and was sentenced to three years in a West End revival of 'Singin' in the rain'.

But of course it couldn't last, by 1978 Cliff was getting increasingly into disco. He changed his name back to Richard and made 'Saturday Night Fever' with Sue Barker. Punk was over, but 'Cliffy Bastard' had made his point.

And that's how it happened.

FIRST AID HINTS

tongue stuck on ice lolly
1 Throw boiling water at ice lolly

decapitation
1 KEEP CALM
2 Hide all incriminating weapons: meat chopper, cheese cutter, executioner's block and axe
3 Go to pub for alibi

Spot the deliberate mistake

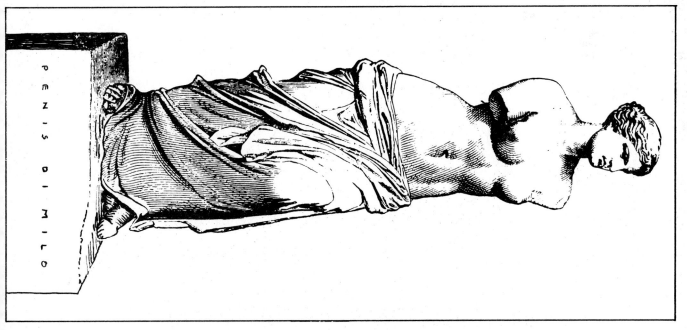

Radical Flower

A traditional arrangement

WHO SAYS FLOWER ARRANGING IS BORING?

Most people do actually, and they're right. Flower arranging is normally mind-numbingly nob-shrinkingly, flap-waggingly tedious. But not for long. Because now thanks to a New Wave of young 'alternative' flower arrangers things are finally changing. It may be hard for the older more conservative generation of bung-'em-in-a-vase-with-some-water artistes to accept but what originally looked like a media-hyped flash in the pan now seems to be here to stay. It is called **CONCEPT FLOWER ARRANGING.**

This arrangement is called ▶ THE DOLE QUEUE. Its latent symbolism is deeply poetic and it will lend political credibility to any dining table.

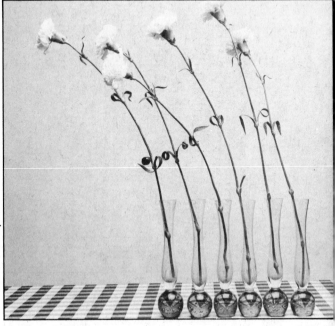

The Dole Queue

Arranging

Bolero

Nuclear War

◀We're all proud of our young athletes, so what could be more thrilling than to have Jayne TORVILL and Christopher DEAN battling for Britain in your very own front room?

Phew! Is this a taste of the ▶ holocaust to come or merely a constant reminder of that fateful day in 1945? It will blow your mind.

Shergar

◀A witty little arrangement. Saves money on flowers too.

A warning about glue ▶ sniffing? A complaint about the price of cocaine or the fact that it's often mixed with flower? Or merely a rather painful way to keep up with the latest trend?

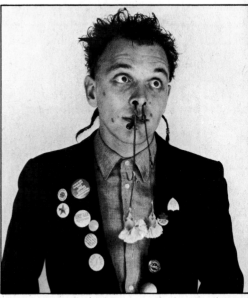

The 1984 Olympics

KNOW YOUR ENEMY

NO 43. PEOPLE YOU HAVE TO SHARE YOUR FRIDGE WITH

● **Type A**
Mr 'Hey look, it's only a sausage' This is the worst bastard of all. He or she will drive you CRAZY by distorting hippy or left wing values in order to excuse himself for ripping off your grub! He will make you feel like a complete, petty, Nazi, possessionist breadhead, because he's eaten all your bacon. He will adopt an INFURIATINGLY reasonable, soft spoken tone and say, 'Look if it *really* means that much to you, I'll buy you some more,' but you know it's fucking midnight and you're hungry *now*. Of course you are more than welcome to help yourself to this guy's stuff, but who wants an empty tube of Craft cheese spread?

● **Type B**
Ms 'Look why don't we have a house kitty and buy a communal sausage' This girl is a complete nuisance. She doesn't realize that Mr 'Hey look, it's only a sausage' will eat it and say 'Hey look, it's only a sausage'.

● **Type C**
Mr and Ms 'Look those sausages are mine and Jackie's' The house couple, and a right pain, they have electric fences and snarling Doberman Pinchers round their neat, well-stocked bit of the fridge. And every night, they

cook themselves PROPER MEALS, like spag bol's and amazingly together things like that, and have YOGHURTS afterwards. They form a united front, and are *totally* unassailable in fridge matters. And then there's a bit of their amazing spag bol left, and you drool a bit, but no, they scrape it into a bowl and put clingfilm over it and go upstairs and make the floorboards creak all through 'The Untouchables'.

Type D
Mr Sticky Label A perfect gent, marks his own stuff clearly, and uses only that . . . Except I could really do with a cup of tea, and she's got loads of milk, if I just pinch a bit . . .

QUESTION: Why did Juliet stab herself in the Capulet tomb?
ANSWER: Because Romeo had eaten her last sausage, despite the fact that it was clearly marked 'J' in biro, and in her part of the FRIDGE.

QUESTION: Why did Delilah cut off all Samson's hair?
ANSWER: Because she caught him using a bit of her milk in his coffee, and all right it was only a splash, but it just seems to happen every single time, and the other night she brought some friends back for coffee, and there wasn't enough milk, which was ridiculous, because she'd only bought it the day before, and there's no way the house can be run if people don't feel confident about leaving private property in the FRIDGE.

QUESTION: Why did Paul McCartney leave Jane Asher for Linda Eastman?
ANSWER: Linda might not be as talented as Jane, but at least she doesn't deliberately peel off the sticky labels marked 'Paul's' that he'd put on the half empty box of fish fingers, in the ice-making compartment of the FRIDGE.

QUESTION: What keeps Cliff and Sue together?
ANSWER: Their fridge is broken.

But don't blame the fridge.

When Napoleon invaded Russia to get his yoghurt back, it wasn't the fridge that had nicked it.

When the 'I hadn't even opened this carton of orange juice' war (later known as 'The Second World War') started, it wasn't the fridge that had drunk the juice. No. *IT WAS THATCHER*

ARE YOU AS COOL AS YOU THINK?

ARE YOU AS YOUNG AS YOU PRETEND TO BE? IS GROOVY YOUR MIDDLE NAME OR IS IT REALLY JEREMY? THE FOLLOWING QUIZ WILL SORT OUT THE SHEEP FROM THE KIDS

1 YOU WOULD MOST LIKE TO ASSASSINATE:
- [ ] **a** Thatcher
- [ ] **b** Hitler
- [ ] **c** Orville

2 AS A CHILD YOU MOST ENJOYED PLAYING WITH:
- [ ] **a** a hula-hoop
- [ ] **b** clickies
- [ ] **c** petrol bombs

3 A NOB IS:
- [ ] **a** something you open a door with
- [ ] **b** a member of the aristocracy
- [ ] **c** a nob

4 YOU REFER TO YOUR RECORD PLAYER AS:
- [ ] **a** my record player
- [ ] **b** the quad I liberated from Curry's during a street fight back in '82
- [ ] **c** Mr Twirly

5 YOU REMEMBER WHEN FIVE PINTS OF BABYCHAM COST:
- [ ] **a** 4/6
- [ ] **b** £1.97
- [ ] **c** two cows and your first born son

6 IS BOB DYLAN:
- [ ] **a** The leading protest singer of our generation?
- [ ] **b** a winter sport?
- [ ] **c** extremely boring?

7 YOU HAVE JUST BEEN RUN OVER BY A BUS. DO YOU:
☐ **a** Shrug it off?
☐ **b** Start crying and wet your pants?
☐ **c** Get a stiffy?

8 YOUR TUTOR GIVES YOU A BAD MARK FOR AN ESSAY. YOU:
☐ **a** poo your pants
☐ **b** poo in your tutor's pants
☐ **c** stab your tutor to death and then poo all over his desk

9 YOU HAVE CHOSEN THE MUSIC FOR YOUR FUNERAL. IT IS:
☐ **a** Itsy Bitsy Teeny Weeny Yellow Polka Dot Bikini by Brian Highland
☐ **b** The theme tune to Upstairs Downstairs
☐ **c** Ra Ra Rasputin by Boney M

10 DID THE CHICKEN CROSS THE ROAD:
☐ **a** To go shoping?
☐ **b** To score some smack off a heavy-weight dealer and rap about Nietzche with William Burroughs?
☐ **c** To avoid the chicken-shagger?

SCORE: 1: a, 3, b, 2, c, 37 **2:** a, 0, b, 0, c, 4½ **3:** a, −56, b, −67, c, 1 **4:** a, 1, b, 3, c, 9 **5:** a, 1, b, 2, c, 3 **6:** a, 0, b, 0, c, 0, d, 0, e, 0, f, 0, g, 0, h, 3 **7:** a, 2, b, 3, c, 0 **8:** a, 0, b, 3, c, −9 **9:** a, 0, b, 0, c, 1 **10:** a, 22, b, 0, c, 14

HOW TO INTERPRET YOUR SCORE THAT IS IF YOU BOTHERED TO WORK IT OUT NERDY FACE.

IF YOU SCORED BETWEEN 0 and 4 (and I'm not talking about chicks – well I wouldn't be really would I, 'cos it would be a really sexist comment all right?)
What a toss-pot bumlicky toilet brain you are. You can't even count properly can you? That's right! ha ha tricked you – because there's no way you could have scored between 0 and 4 so there.

IF YOU SCORED BETWEEN 4 and 35
Square. Geriatric. Nazi. What are you doing reading a book like this? Why don't you just go out and join the Monday Club on your way to collect your pension? Or perhaps they don't do things like that in Chislehurst, I don't think.

EVERYONE ELSE
You think you're pretty cool, don't you? Well you're wrong – because the most nerdy-brained thing you can do is to take a quiz seriously. So who's wearing the sticky pants now?

Genesis of a Rebel

Way way back in '76 when John Cooper Smellybum came to me and said, 'How can I be a great poet like you?' The first thing I said was, 'Change your name.' So he changed his name to Clark, and it was as Clark Cooper Smellybum that he was knocked over and killed by a bus, on his way to his first ever gig. Which just goes to show that the world of poetry is a wild dangerous one, and even knowing me won't necessarily get you across the road, and why the bloody hell should it! Who do you think I am? The Green Cross man?

It was this experience that led me to partially forsake the world of punk poetry and invent **NEW WAVE COMEDY**

Here are some examples of New Wave jokes.

Q: Why did the chicken cross the road?
A: To protest against Cruise missiles.

A: My dog's got no nob.
B: Your dog's got no nob? How does it make love?
A: It's a bitch

A: Knock knock
B: Who's there?
A: Thatcher

Those were some very right on jokes. And they were **BRILLIANT.**

In order to be a really brilliant New Wave comedian like me, you need three things; legs, a mouth, and a bottom.

LEGS: For running on (and off) the stage.
MOUTH: For telling the New Wave jokes, and swearing (to look hard).
BOTTOM: For dissipation of pre 'gig' nerves.

My first ever gig ('gig' is New Wave comedy slang for drinking eight pints of lager and then standing up in front of people and being sworn at and then coming off and drinking more lager and asking your mates if it was racist to use the words 'garden shed' in the fourth joke. 'Joke' is New Wave comedy slang for ... bloody cripes, I think we'd better have a glossary.)

NEW WAVE COMEDY GLOSSARY

'Punchline'—punchlines can only be spotted in retrospect. If a sudden silence of awed disbelief descends on the audience followed almost immediately by a violent barrage of obscene abuse, then whatever the comedian said immediately before that, was a 'punchline'.
'Lager'—wages.
'Joke'—bloody cripes, I think we'd better have a glossary.

My first ever gig was absolutely brilliant. I'll tell you how it happened. I'd come down to London from my parents. Now wandering round London that day, I came across this big cathedral called St Paul's, and I thought, 'I know, I'll do a gag about St Paul's Cathedral.' So I shouted, 'Hey everybody, I've got a nob as big as St Paul's Cathedral!' *IT WAS BRILLIANT*!! And there wasn't even anyone watching! That's how New Wave comedy was invented.

FUTURE GROOVING:

Hi there. If you're a seasoned groover like me, then lots of people probably keep trying to eat you! (BRILLIANT) But seriously, do you view your future grooving with relish – or with ketchup! (I JUST CAN'T STOP! I'M A CRAZY WILD YOUNG THING! HONESTLY, I HAVEN'T A *CLUE* WHAT I'LL DO NEXT) Here's a guide to what will be groovy between 1984 and 1990, and what will be totally square.
Remember: **It's a piece of piss to be groovy, but it's not groovy to be a piece of piss.**

GROOVY '84-'90	NOT GROOVY '84-'90
Cliff Richard	*Flared trousers*
Being cool	*Being square*
Pop music	*Ballroom dancing and war*
New wave poetry/comedy/music etc	*Voting conservative*
Anarchy	*Pooing your pants at a gig by accident*

I'VE GOT AN ABSOLUTE WHOPPER RIGHT HERE IN MY TROUSERS

A spy story by Rick.

'Bloody crikey,' mused 'Raunchy' Rick, super spy, 'Now I'm bound to get caught and London will be drowned in a sea of Doctor Wang's molten snot.' It was departure lounge 'A' at Heathrow Airport and Rick had been caught up in an infernal customs' 'spot check'. The seconds ticked by.

'You next,' barked the officer. 'Any spots?'

'What you see on my face, plus a few on my chest and inner thighs,' said Rick, casually, 'and could you hurry up please, I've got to save England.'

'Oh yeah, what about your botty, Snotty?' said Hitler.

And that's why Rick had mused 'bloody crikey' because Rick knew that right bang on his botty was an enormous false bum boil, containing explosives, secret plans, three litres of table wine and a packet of comedy 'johnnies' that he'd been looking forward to showing off in the Union bar.

Rick thought quickly.

'Yes, since you come to mention it,' he shouted, 'I've got an absolute bursting whopper right in my trousers.'

But at this very moment, gorgeous Sabrina the air hostess strolled by.

'It's bigger than this airport,' screamed Rick, 'and if you touch it, it'll go off.' The plan worked; Hitler had heard enough; the last thing he wanted was burst spot all over his nice, nazi uniform and 'Marvellous Maggie' badge, so he let Rick through.

'Thank blimey,' thought Rick, as he hurried off to the taxi rank, 'now to stop Doctor Wang.'

But Sabrina had different ideas.

'OK big boy, I've heard the advert, now let's sample the goods,' she drawled (and this was a *real* girly, don't forget, not Vyvyan in a dress).

CAPTAIN PARANOIA

'Who's that tapping at the window?
Who's that knocking at the door?
What's that face in the darkness?
What's that creeping cross the floor?
Police? Parents? Pregnant?
Never felt like this before.
Come on now, tell me who's oui there!
"Hi Kids, Captain Paranoia".'

When you're walking alone down a street and you see a copper, the Captain's with you, it's him that makes you feel guilty, even if you haven't done anything.

You take the Captain to a party, it's him telling you you're the most boring person there, it's him who makes you certain that you're making the least interesting contribution. Why is everyone else so confident? Why do they seem so happy? Why? Because you can't hear what the Captain's saying to *them.*

On your birthday, the Captain squeezes himself through the letterbox with your cards and whispers, 'Go on, count 'em' so you do, and there aren't very many, and it's then that the Captain points out how few real friends you've got, and how much you'd love to be popular, like *everyone else.*

In the bank, the Captain's at the head of the queue, shouting, 'Hey kids, the *other* queues are moving faster, those *other* people are *pushing in.'*

It's the Captain who tells you that everyone else has done loads and loads of work for the exam and you haven't done *any.*

It's the Captain who tells you other people get paid more than you.

It's the Captain who whispers in foolish ears, 'People on the dole live in luxury.'

NEVER FORGET. CAPTAIN PARANOIA IS A BASTARD. AND HE VOTES CONSERVATIVE.

Right on Mike! Tell it like it is.

GETTING A BA

THE FAX

Almost everyone would like to be a famous and successful rock star, but out of 3 billion people in the world only 439 have achieved this ambition. A somewhat depressing statistic you might think—and you might be right. But before you let the squares at your careers office sign you up for a YOP scheme in double-glazing, ask yourself these questions.

1 Am I as sexy as Simon le Bon/The dark-haired girl in Bananarama?

2 Do girls/boys have to wash their pants a lot after seeing me? (You might have to ask the lady in the launderette to verify this one).

3 Do I own a guitar/microphone/drumkit/bass/synthesiser/amplifier?

4 If so, can I work it properly?

5 Have I got any friends with rich parents who live in a big detached mansion with its own recording studio and no neighbours within three miles?

6 Am I good at taking drugs?

7 Do I have a recording contract?

If the answer to most of these questions is 'Yes', then you are an overprivileged bag of horse shit. If the answer is 'No', don't despair completely. Just despair a bit and

crappy old hippy

maybe attempt suicide really badly as come to think of it this is quite a good way to get a lot of sympathy espesh from Mater and Pater who might well decide to buy you the Fender you've always hankered after.

The next thing essential for all aspiring pop stars is to learn the language of the Rock world, or Rockspeak as it is better known.

Here are some examples:

axe	**A & R man**
gig	**rider**
stack	**liggers**
roadie	**rim shot**
NME	**net profit**
amp	**venue**

Always use at least four of these words in every sentence whenever addressing anyone associated with the pop world: press, managers, artistes, groupies—otherwise you will have ZERO CREDIBILITY. 'The liggers ripped off the rider while the roadie was sussing out my axe problem after the gig' sounds a lot more impressive than 'Clive's friends drank all the light ale while Jeremy's brother was trying to fix my guitar after the Chess Society beano'.

So now you've got the equipment and can speak the lingo. All that remains is to get some like-minded friends together, develop

number from 6?

1

an image, write a lot of very catchy tunes, do a demo tape, get a distribution deal, an agent, a manager and a record label, sell a lot of singles, appear on Top of the Pops, sell a lot of albums and get some framed platinum discs to hang in your loo, leave your wife/husband/girlfriend/boyfriend, leave your manager, get a famous person to get photographed having sex with you, take a lot of drugs, sue your ex-manager, sue your record company, smash up some photographers at an airport, develop a drink problem, buy a football club, get arrested somewhere exotic, meet Princess Anne, do a TV ad for a soft drink, have a car crash, go to a health farm, do a cameo role in a Bond film, split with your new wife/husband/girl-friend/boyfriend, split with your new manager, record company, the rest of the group, buy a stately home, put on weight, write a song about Beirut/Soweto/a dead rock star, die.

You have now arrived and can tell everyone stories about the careers master who told you you should settle for something safe like double-glazing. EASY ISN'T IT?

(If any famous rock stars are reading this—hello, I've always been a terrific fan of yours. If Stewart Copeland is reading this—Hi Stew, I think you're the best and I was wondering if you have any cymbals you don't want any more and perhaps could slip my way—anyway you must be a millionaire by now so why not just buy me some new ones, you bastard!).

rip it off for loads of cash and do straight into the charts at number 5

The history of POP

PART FIVE

ELECTROPOP

London, 1942. The height of the blitz.

2nd Lt Cliff Richard stood before them, a shy gangly youth of some twenty summers who, when he moved, still showed the clean limbed strength and grace of a young boy, while in his eyes could be seen already the weariness of a man who has seen too much of this wicked world, too soon.

'Permission to speak, sir?' said Cliff, and when he spoke, it was pure big band! It was almost as if Glenn Miller stood in the room beside him, conducting the massed ranks of musicians in some of Cliff's greatest and best loved songs: 'In the Mood', 'Pennsylvania Six, Five Thousand', how many more would there have been had not Cliff's country needed him so?

'What's that huge thing the size of a house you've got there?' snapped Peabody. Cliff steeled himself for the tirade he knew he must face, he'd been warned so often about his sloppy uniforms.

'I'm sorry sir,' he stammered, 'but I simply cannot find trousers that will contain it.'

'No no, not your nob,' roared Peabody. 'That enormous square thing.'

'That is what I wished to see you about sir, it is the world's first computer.'

Peabody could scarcely believe his ears. He glanced at Churchill's note and then again at the machine.

'That's it!' he spat, 'that's Enigma.' Stepping carefully over Cliff's nob he approached the computer.

'Show me how it works, Lieutenant,' he screamed.

And there and then Cliff sat down and played 'Are Friends Electric' and 'Doctor Doctor'.

Out of the white hot furnace of war, Electropop was born.

'Hallo, Prime Minister?' hissed Peabody into the telephone. 'We've got something down here that forty-five years from now will dominate the charts and bore everyone pooey. Shall we use it on the Germans?'

'Shakin' Stevens is a personal friend of mine!' said Churchill, hanging up.

And that's how it happened.

NEVER MIND THE SEX PISTOLS, HERE'S OUR BOLLOCKS

What is this? Fascists!!! I suppose you think our rudies are too hot to handle??

NEIL: Er, right, er, power Mr Bowie, look will you not keep pushing OK, like, I paid for this seat you know, I mean actually personally laid out the bread... Oh not you David, I'm just talking to this crazed animal beside me in the Motorhead T shirt – Look Vyvyan will you just *mellow out*, OK! Anyway Mr Bowie, er, yeah, power, er, how does it feel to have so much bread?

BOWIE: Let's dance, put on your red shoes and dance the blues, let's dance –

NEIL: Well like obviously it's nice of you to ask me, but you see, I have to lay down this interview, for our book, or else, like Vyvyan will just draw lots of repressive cartoons of his thingy on it. So anyway, like why do you never play at Glastonbury, or the Stonehenge solstice?

BOWIE: Ziggy played guitar, jiving good with Weird and Gilly and the spiders from Mars, he played it left hand, but played it too far, became the special man, but boy could he play guitar –

NEIL: You're deliberately avoiding

INTERVIEW

answering the question man. Now I don't want to put on my like heavy duty interviewer hat but ... Vyvyan! Please don't wee in my bag! My stash is in there! Please! Oh no, ten quid's worth of 'Shetland Brown' – soaked.

VYVYAN: Sorry Neil, but there's 18,000 people queuing for the bog and someone's taken a book in.

NEIL: I bet I'm the only head in the whole concert who's going to have to take his stash home and put it on top of the radiator.

VYVYAN: How's the interview going?

NEIL: Well, he's being a bit evasive.

VYVYAN: Oy, David! Is it true you flirted with nazi ideology during your Heroes period?

BOWIE: As they pulled you out of the oxygen tent, you asked for the latest party.

VYVYAN: Yeah, I see what you mean Neil, he's not answering the questions is he?

NEIL: Oh no, the tape's running –

bowie

'**Workers of the world unite! You have nothing to lose but your chains**' Cliff Richard

'**She's a devil woman, with evil on her mind**' Karl Marx

'**I am, and always have been, a nazi, I am not ashamed**' Mrs Thatcher

'**My nob's bigger than Heathrow Airport**' John Noakes

'**Oooh blimey Rick, I don't half fancy you, want a bonk?**' Felicity Kendall

All power to the Soviets, peace, bread, freedom' Cliff Richard

'**Daddy's home**' Lenin

'**I do wish John wouldn't keep lying about the size of his nob**' Mrs Noakes

'**If I had a pound, for every unemployed person, I'd have about five quid less than I've actually got**' Michael Heseltine

'**Cor Rick, I'd like to get inside your trousers!**' Isla St Clair

'**I am a complete and utter bastard**' Mrs Thatcher

'**I'm telling you, my nob is bigger than Heathrow airport**' John Noakes

'**Religion is the opium of the masses**' Cliff Richard

'**Crap! I went to church once, rubbish, no buzz at all**' Neil

'**And I'm telling you it's not, I've seen it matey, and it's tiny**' Mrs Noakes

'**Seig Heil**' Mrs Thatcher

'**All right then, bloody go and get the tape measure you bitch**' John Noakes

'**All right, I will**' Mrs Noakes

'**Free Nelson Mandela**' Cliff Richard

'**There, you see, one and a half inches**' Mrs Noakes

'**One and three bloody quarters!**' John Noakes

'**Well even if it is one and threequarters, that's still not as big as Heathrow airport**' Mrs Noakes

'**Erect! I was talking about erect!**' John Noakes

'**Are you trying to say that it's going to expand from 1¼ inches, to 20 or 30 square miles, just by thinking dirty?**' Mrs Noakes

'**It might**' John Noakes

'**And it might bloody not**' Mrs Noakes

'**Er look, I don't want to get heavy or anything, but could you like stop going on about John's nob on our quotes page?**' Neil

'**Yeah, we're sick to death of hearing about your todger**' Vyvyan

'**Size doesn't matter anyway, everyone knows that, although I'm not saying mine isn't enormous, because it is**' Rick

'**Size does matter if it's bigger than Heathrow Airport**' Mrs Noakes

'**Which it is**' John Noakes

'**SHUT UP ABOUT IT**' Rick, Vyvyan, Mike and Neil

ACKNOWLEDGEMENTS

Many, many thanks to: **Ade Edmondson**
Nigel Planer
Christopher Ryan
and especially to **Paul Jackson**

Editor: **Terence Blacker**
Designer: **Neville Brody**
Assistant: **Valerie Hawthorn**
Photographer: **Sheila Rock**
Assistant: **Amanda Searle**
Make-up: **Miranda Boyer**
Illustrations: **Neville Brody, Rik Mayall, Lise Mayer**
Typesetting: **The Printed Word**
Picture credits: **Prince Charles** (Rex Features), **Ronald Reagan** (Associated Press), **Hotair balloon** (Rex Features), **Trotsky** (Mary Evans), **Neil hitching on the road** (Caroline Blacker), **Koo Stark** (Rex Features), **Bowie interview** (London Features International), **Venus DiMilo** (Mary Evans)
Lyrics from **Power to all our friends** *reproduced by kind permission of Big Secret Music Ltd and those for* **Congratulations** *by kind permission of P. Maurice Music Co/KPM.*
Props buyer and picture researcher: **Morven Blair**

And special thanks to:

Jenne Casarotto, Aude Powell, Viv Riley, Robin Stubbs, Ian Hatfield, Kate, Roland, Alexei and Linda.